D0498395

Faith No More

Faith No More
Why People Reject Religion

———∽∾———

Phil Zuckerman

OXFORD
UNIVERSITY PRESS

OXFORD
UNIVERSITY PRESS

Oxford University Press, Inc., publishes works that further
Oxford University's objective of excellence
in research, scholarship, and education.

Oxford   New York
Auckland   Cape Town   Dar es Salaam   Hong Kong   Karachi
Kuala Lumpur   Madrid   Melbourne   Mexico City   Nairobi
New Delhi   Shanghai   Taipei   Toronto

With offices in
Argentina   Austria   Brazil   Chile   Czech Republic   France   Greece
Guatemala   Hungary   Italy   Japan   Poland   Portugal   Singapore
South Korea   Switzerland   Thailand   Turkey   Ukraine   Vietnam

Published by Oxford University Press, Inc.
198 Madison Avenue, New York, New York 10016

www.oup.com

Oxford is a registered trademark of Oxford University Press

Library of Congress Cataloging-in-Publication Data
Zuckerman, Phil.
Faith no more : why people reject religion / Phil Zuckerman.
p.   cm.
Includes bibliographical references and index.
ISBN 978-0-19-974001-7 (acid-free paper)
1. Apostasy—Christianity.   2. Ex-church members—United States.   3. Non-church-affiliated
people—United States.   4. Atheism—United States.   5. United States—Church
history—21st century.   6. Religion and sociology—United States.   I. Title.
BR517.Z83 2011
277.3'083—dc22   2011007917

4732 7647 11/11

1 3 5 7 9 8 6 4 2

Printed in the United States of America
on acid-free paper

CONTENTS

ACKNOWLEDGMENTS

I would like to thank Pitzer College for several grants that helped support the research for this book. I would also like to thank my graduate research assistant, Kerri Blumenthal, as well as my undergraduate research assistants: Alexandria A. Bannerman, Erin Caliri, David R. Casler, Sasha Cohen, Cassandra Cona, Amanda J. Curtis, Melanie H. Epstein, Maxamilien Fortgang, Sylvie Froncek, Sophia Galano, Jyoti Gautam, Samuel Greene, Alejandra Gillette-Teran, Sophie Goodwin, Jerry Johnson, Rhonda Kruschen, Steven Losco, Korin Nadelle, Morgan Peterkin, Jonny Robertson, Travis Luke Rooke-Ley, and Brittni Stenmo.

I am also indebted to my colleagues: Ryan Falcioni, Luke Galen, Sandy Hamilton, Shayne Lee, Peter Nardi, John Norvell, Frank Pasquale, and James Spickard.

Finally, my earnest gratitude goes out to Theo Calderara, Dan Burke, Gary Cienmarcos, Marvin Zuckerman, and Stacy Elliott.

Faith No More

oⅣɔ

Introduction

A wind of secularity is currently blowing across North America. No one can predict the overall course of this wind— whether it will gain speed in the years ahead or eventually run its course and peter out. But for now, it is blowing quite steadily. The growth of irreligion in the United States in recent years is undeniable. According to sociologists Barry Kosmin and Ariela Keysar, the increase in the number of Americans eschewing religion in recent years "has been one of the most important trends on the American religious scene."[1]

Surveys tell much of the story. According to the American Religious Identification Survey, 15% of Americans now claim "none" as their religion, up from 8% back in 1990—a near doubling of "nones" in 20 years. These findings were supported by the Pew Forum's U.S. Religious Landscape Survey, which reports that 16% of Americans are religiously "unaffiliated." According to the Harris Poll, in 2003, 4% of Americans were atheist, in 2006 it was 6%, and in 2008, the number was 10%— with another 9% being agnostic. These are the highest rates of atheism/agnosticism ever reported in an American survey. Finally, a 2009 survey undertaken by the nationally syndicated *Parade* magazine found that 27% of Americans "do not practice any religion" and 22% said that religion was "not a factor" in their lives. Again, these are the highest levels of secularity among Americans ever seen.[2]

The recent growth of secularity in the United States is evident in other ways as well. There has been a slew of best-selling books in the last few years that are highly critical of religion, namely Sam Harris's *The End of Faith* (2004), Christopher Hitchens's *God Is Not Great* (2007), and Richard Dawkins's *The God Delusion* (2006). Additionally, there has been a notable growth recently among atheist groups in America, such as the Freedom from Religion Foundation, which reported an unprecedented 25% membership increase in 2006 alone. The Secular Student Alliance—a college campus group for nonbelievers—now claims over 200 chapters nationwide, up from 42 in 2003. And secularity has skyrocketed among younger Americans, of which the percentage of religious "nones" is estimated to be somewhere between 30% and 40%. One recent study found that only 53% of Americans born after 1981 believe in God.[3]

This increase in irreligion is not occurring because secular people are having a ton of babies. Quite the contrary; it is the strongly religious who have the most kids. In fact, compared to all religious groups, nonreligious people are the least likely to have lots of children. This means that most of the nonreligious people in America today were actually raised with some religion, and then at a certain point, they opted out. They rejected their religion. They became apostates. Thus, in the words of social psychologists Bruce Hunsberger and Bob Altemeyer, the "real story" underlying the increase of secularity in North America is "the growth in apostasy."[4]

The word "apostasy" comes from the Greek "apostasia," which means "a defection or revolt." Benjamin Beit-Hallahmi defines apostasy as "disaffection, defection, alienation, disengagement, and disaffiliation from a religious group." David Caplovitz and Fred Sherrow define apostasy as "the relinquishing of a set of religious beliefs" but add that apostasy involves "not only a loss of faith, but rejection of a particular ascriptive community as a basis for self-identification." David Bromley succinctly defines apostates as "individuals who once held a religious identity but no longer do so."[5]

Just as with religiosity, there are various forms or types of apostasy. Armand Mauss has put forth a three-type classification, based on the reasons that underlie individuals' withdrawal from religion: intellectual apostasy (they just don't believe anymore), social apostasy (a disintegration of social bonds with coreligionists or the formation of social ties outside one's religious community), and emotional apostasy (one has psychological reactions to perceived church hypocrisy, or one comes to apostasy as an outgrowth of an unhappy family life). Merlin Brinkerhoff and Kathryn Burke offer another three-type classification: "ritualists" who have lost some or all of their religious beliefs, but continue to identify with a religious community and still participate in various ceremonies and rituals, "outsiders" who still maintain clear religious beliefs but no longer identify with a religious community, and finally "true apostates," those who have both lost their religious beliefs and become totally disaffiliated from a religious community.[6]

Based on my own analysis of interviews with 87 people who were once religious but are no longer, I can offer my own typology of apostasy. First, in acknowledgment of *when* in the course of his or her life an individual rejects religion, we can make a distinction between *early* apostasy and *late* apostasy. The former refers to individuals who were raised in a religious home and were socialized into a religious identity as children without much of a conscious choice in the matter, who then go on to reject that religion as soon as they became teenagers or young adults. In other words, they shed their religion once they were no longer under the direct influence of their families. This type of apostasy is closely linked to an individual's general maturation process, of growing up and finding one's own individuality, fashioning one's own identity, and rebelling against or simply rejecting certain elements of one's parents' lives or beliefs—of which religion may often be a part. Early apostasy is quite common among the nonreligious. For instance, in a study of members of secular-humanistic groups in the Pacific Northwest, Frank Pasquale found that the majority of people knew they were nonreligious by the time they were 22, and in fact 25% of them knew they were nonreligious in their teenage years. In contrast to early apostasy, late apostasy refers to individuals who adopted their religion on their own as adults, not because they were raised to be religious by their parents. Their religiosity was thus not a direct result of childhood socialization but of a conscious choice made as mature, unfettered adults. And then, such individuals subsequently abandon their religion much later in life. What makes late apostasy qualitatively different from early apostasy is the fact that it isn't as interwoven or interconnected with the general process of growing up and creating one's own identity outside of family influence. Late apostasy, admittedly, is quite rare. It is far more typical for people who were raised in a certain religious tradition to reject it in their late teens or early adulthood.[7]

There is also the matter of just how deeply an individual's rejection of his or her religion goes. That is, we can make a distinction between *shallow* apostasy and *deep* apostasy. Shallow apostasy refers to the phenomenon of people rejecting their religion but who still consider themselves to be strongly spiritual, or at least not wholly or completely secular. They may not believe in Jesus as the Messiah anymore, but they may still consider him to be a special, moral teacher worthy of respect and reverence. They may not believe in the God of the Bible anymore, but they still think that there is "something" out there, some supernatural force of love or sacred unity that upholds and permeates the universe. They may not belong to a church anymore, but they don't mind going to a religious service once in a while, especially around the holidays. While such individuals have rejected a specific religion and have experienced a weakening of faith, they are not totally secular. They may have no problem calling themselves ex-Catholic or ex-Mormon, but they are simultaneously not comfortable calling themselves atheists. Deep apostasy refers to individuals whose break from religion is total and absolute; they no longer consider themselves religious in any way, shape, or form. Nor do they consider themselves spiritual. They are convinced nonbelievers and are totally uninterested in participating in anything religious. They are positively secular, through and through. The main point to be gleaned from the distinction between shallow and deep apostasy is that not all apostates end up in the same place. The depth of their rejection of religion varies significantly. While many of the men and women interviewed for this study do classify themselves as confirmed atheists, many others do not. Many classified themselves as open-minded agnostics, believers in "something out there," Buddhists, and so on. Others, particularly those who had been raised as Jews, Mormons, and Catholics, considered themselves to be still somehow culturally linked to their religious tradition, even though they are no longer true believers. The individuals interviewed for this study were about evenly divided between deep and shallow apostates.

Finally, there is the matter of just how truly significant or personally transformative the shift from religiosity to secularity is for given individuals. While all 87 apostates that I interviewed withdrew from religion, not everyone was as strong in his or her religious convictions or religious identification to begin with—so the withdrawal from religion took on greater or lesser significance, depending on how religious the person originally had been. The distinction here is between *mild* apostasy and *transformative* apostasy. The former refers to individuals who rejected religion but weren't all that religious in the first place; the religion he or she rejected was never that significant a part of life, so letting it go wasn't all that big of a deal, entailing few personal consequences, little social disruption, and no real psychological turmoil. Transformative apostasy refers to the phenomenon of individuals who were deeply, strongly religious who then went on to reject their religion. For such people, apostasy is a true personal revolution, a life-altering transformation. It involves not only a massive psychological reorientation from a religious to a secular worldview, but it also often entails a loss of close friendships, alienation from a strong community, and even rejection by one's family.

While these three dimensions of apostasy—early/late, shallow/deep, mild/transformative—manifest themselves in various combinations, it is the stories of deep and transformative apostasy that are obviously the most dramatic. One such apostate is Nathan. He is a 42-year-old African American who was raised in Philadelphia but who now lives in Alabama, where he is a college professor. Religion was central to Nathan's family life and his personal identity when he was growing up. For his first 27 years, he was devoted, committed, enveloped, and engrossed in all aspects of religion.

> *I was really active in the church....I got really serious as far as religion....I mean, my worldview was totally that God is in control of everything.*

Nathan attended his family's Pentecostal church several times a week, he prayed constantly, and he was so enthusiastically devout that his family referred to him as their "own little Jesus." After high school, Nathan attended Oral Roberts University, majoring in church ministries and evangelism. He started up a prison ministry, where students could preach the word of God to inmates at nearby prisons. During his summers, he went on missions to Jamaica and Mexico. He even spent one summer riding the subways of New York City, preaching the word of God to anyone who would listen. After graduating, he attended graduate school at Trinity Evangelical Divinity School and Regent University—both strongly Christian institutions. A master of both Old and New Testaments, a servant of Jesus Christ, a man of God, a convinced believer—Nathan's entire life was his faith and his church and his Bible.

And then, the doubts and questions seeped in, little by little, over the course of several years. For a long time he countered them with earnest prayer and even greater piety. He overcame the seeping skepticism by engrossing himself ever deeper in his religious studies and his church. But the questions and doubts persisted.

For Pentecostal Christians, the ability of God to heal is central. Nathan had believed in God's healing powers all his life. Then one day, it finally occurred to him that he never actually saw any proof of miraculous healing. He saw the very opposite:

> I remember the day that I rejected Christianity.... It's weird...but one day I was driving to the gym to work out and I thought about a good buddy of mine who was in a wheelchair. He was a brilliant guy. I thought to myself: "If Rick ever got up out of that wheelchair, it would be on CNN.... If a blind person got healed, it would be on CNN." I watch CNN every day, and I've never seen a story about a paralyzed person or blind person...so then I thought: God doesn't heal. I had already kind of come to that conclusion, but this way of thinking in terms of it is a fact in my mind that the God of the scriptures that claims to be a healer does not heal today.... Then I concluded that if God doesn't heal, then the God of the Bible does not exist. If the God of the Bible does not exist, then I don't believe in God. It was really that simple.

For Nathan, the transition was extremely difficult. It was a solo journey, for which he had no road map and no comrades. No one in his family could understand his rejection of Christianity. His parents were quite worried about his apostasy, and they continue to pray that it is merely a phase that he will soon pull out of. Most of his friends were unsympathetic, worried, disappointed. And when Nathan goes out on dates now, he finds that his irreligiosity is often a "deal breaker."

Life for Nathan as a new apostate clearly entailed a dramatic change:

> I had to learn how to be a non-Christian. There was a lot of sort of angst in that. Here I am now, 26 years old, 27—I don't remember the exact age—and I've been pretty much a Christian all that time. A serious Christian. So I have to now learn...there was a lot of sorrow in the fact that I now was in a world, a dangerous world, where I didn't feel I was protected by anything, where I was on my own and things were just kind of random.... So I had to kind of like learn this new worldview. So on the one hand there was a lot of angst and frustration and a lot of—but that didn't last long. The freedom, the tremendous freedom overcame the frustration—the sorrow and the loss, I overcame it because I'm a free thinker.... Here I am now, I can be whatever I want, I can

re-invent myself, I can do whatever I want, I can create my own moral system, and I don't think I ever looked back. I got to the point where I really embraced the freedom, I never looked back. So this period of frustration, of loss of regret, of how am I going to make it . . . was superseded by the tremendous, almost worship of freedom. . . . I worship freedom now instead of God.

People like Nathan are rare. But they certainly exist—now more than ever. What do we actually know about such people? Social scientific research on those who have rejected their religion is actually quite minimal. As Stan Albrecht has noted, "religious leave-taking has received far less attention than has religious conversion."[8] However, from the handful of sporadic studies that have appeared over the past 50 years, certain findings have been consistently reported. For example, apostasy rates are higher among men than women. Apostates are also more likely to be left-leaning politically than non-apostates. Finally, apostates are more likely to be better educated, to get higher grades, and to describe themselves as having an "intellectual orientation" than their religious peers.

That men are more likely to become apostates than women aligns well with a much broader pattern, one supported by a significant body of research: men tend to be less religious than women over all, on every measure of religiosity and in all societies for which we have data.[9] This may be the result of innate genetic or physiological predispositions, different patterns of childhood socialization, or different levels of wealth, power, status, agency, or prestige within society. As for apostasy being strongly correlated with left-leaning, progressive, or radical political views—this too conforms with a broader trend: secular people in general tend to be more liberal and progressive than their religious peers, being less likely to support the death penalty, the War in Iraq, the governmental use of torture, and more likely to support Democratic candidates, women's equality, and gay rights.[10] One has to wonder: does rejecting religion lead people to hold left-wing political values, or is it the other way around—that holding left-wing political values leads people to become apostates? Or are both caused by some third, as-yet unidentified factor? While we can't be sure, what seems plausible is that people who question the official teachings of their religion are probably more comfortable questioning other "official versions of reality."[11] Hence, those who don't feel comfortable accepting the power of religious authorities are probably less likely to accept the political powers that be. And conversely, it seems plausible that people who question the status quo are suspicious of political leaders; are concerned with inequality, power dynamics, and corruption as they exist in the wider society; and might also be sensitive to such things as they play out in religious institutions, leading to an increase of skepticism and doubt. Finally, as for apostasy being strongly correlated with intellectualism, higher education, or as Bob Altemeyer and Bruce Hunsberger have stated, being "very bright," this pattern is also consistent with a larger body of research showing that education appears to have a corrosive effect on religiosity in general. Indeed, higher education has been positively correlated with atheism and secularity in many other studies.[12] High educational attainment probably makes it more difficult to maintain a strong belief in one's religion when learning about the social construction of religion, the history of religious development, the diversity of religious claims, and the inability of many religious claims to be supported by scientific verification. Also, attending college often means meeting people with other viewpoints, which can undermine one's ability to maintain allegiance to a specific set of religious ideals. Furthermore, attending college is often a time away from one's family and childhood friends, thereby loosening social bonds that otherwise might keep tendencies toward apostasy in check.

While the above research is important, it does have its shortcomings. Nearly all of the studies ever published on apostasy over the past 50 years are based on samples made up solely of college students. Therefore, I made sure that the majority of people I interviewed were no longer in college but were older and at different ages and stages in life. A second shortcoming of previous research on apostasy is that the majority of studies were based on survey data, wherein people answered short questions with limited responses available, filling out forms wherein they checked a box or filled in a bubble. Such survey data, while very informative, can often be extremely narrow. Answers tend to be shallow and information tends to be truncated so as to be easily quantified. However, as Janet Jacobs revealed in her pioneering study about people who left new religious movements, apostasy is a story that takes place in a person's life. It involves a "before" period when one is religious, a "during" period at which time a person is in the process of rejection, and an "after" period, when a person is living as a nonreligious individual. Stories of apostasy are also idiosyncratic in terms of the specific causes and personal consequences. Apostasy is a story indeed, and stories just aren't very amenable to survey analysis. For most people, their apostasy is larger, more colorful, more personal, and often more complex than that which can be captured or measured by a short questionnaire. Thus, in our growing understanding of apostasy, what is needed to enrich, embellish, and deepen the existing survey data is data based on in-depth interviews, wherein people have the chance, with the extended time that an open-ended conversation allows, to convey their stories of how and why they rejected their religion.

Such stories are extremely valuable. As sociologist Kirk Hadaway declared some 20 years ago:

> We still do not know enough about why people become apostates.... Perhaps the most fruitful direction for further research in this area would be case histories...of apostates....Though complex, such data would add valuable information to our understanding of the process through which persons reject religion.[13]

This book is an attempt to heed Kirk Hadaway's call for the accumulation, presentation, and analysis of case histories of apostates. I've sat down and talked with people who have rejected their religion, and in listening to their stories, I've tried to learn something about their journey from religiosity to secularity. My analysis is thus based upon the often compelling stories of apostasy as conveyed to me by 87 individuals who were once religious but are no longer. These individuals come from and/or live in various parts of the United States, have a range of ages from the late teens to the late seventies, and represent a diversity of racial, ethnic, and class backgrounds.[14]

Of course, I am well aware that asking people to explain their own loss of faith is not without its methodological shortcomings. Individuals' own recollections of their personal life stories can be unavoidably biased. As Daniel Carson Johnson has pointed out, "apostate accounts are essentially autobiographies, and autobiographies are never perfect works of non-fiction."[15] When looking back on their lives in an attempt to explain their present identities, some men and women may have a tendency to highlight certain details and downplay others—even unconsciously—so as to paint a picture of themselves that makes them comfortable with their current life choices. Some people may inadvertently reconstruct events or embellish memories so that they are not accurate. Others may not even truly know why they are apostates; if Freud taught us anything, it is that people are not always completely or fully aware of their own motives and they are not always readily cognizant of the underlying sources of their decisions. While recognizing these potential pitfalls that come with relying upon people's personal accounts of their own life stories as data, I still think that the best way to find out why people reject religion is to ask those individuals that have actually done so—to get the story directly from the horse's mouth, so to speak.

1

⌒∿⌒

Mother Was an Exorcist

L ike all kids, Robert had nightmares. But his may have been more frequent and more severe than most kids. Robert often dreamt about Satan and his fiery minions breaking into his house, flying up the stairway, and bursting right into his bedroom to rip him to shreds. But that's not the worst part. What makes Robert's case exceptional, and glaringly painful, was the way his parents—specifically, his mother—responded to them. When Robert woke up screaming from a nightmare, his mother didn't comfort him by saying his nightmares were nothing to be afraid of. She didn't tell him that it was all "just a bad dream." Rather, she told him that they weren't dreams at all but were actually true occurrences and that what he was seeing, sensing, and fearing were sober perceptions of a very real, very terrifying threat. As he was screaming in terror at the peak of one of his terrible nightmares, his mother would rush into his room and confirm that, yes, Satan's devils had in fact been there, they actually had been after Robert, and he was lucky that she was there to chase them away.

As Robert explained:

"Oh, there's a demon!" she'd say and, "Oh there's another!" She would call them out and she could see them—or at least tell that they had been there. So

it wasn't like Satan was coming up the stairs in a dream—he actually was coming up the stairs to come and kill me and good thing she caught it! So she would call it out and say, basically, "It's a good thing I got here when I did because this would have been the end of you." So just completely legitimizing the entire—just fearful—saying, of course: "This is what happens because we're the warriors and we're the ones in this neighborhood taking care of everything and getting rid of all the demons, so we're the primary targets"— that kind of thing. So she would do this whole ceremony basically of just, you know, casting them out and whatever—and sometimes she would say: "Well, you just need to tell them, you know, in the name of Jesus by the blood of Christ you need to get out of here. This is a Christian home and the demons need to get out of here."

After chasing away the demons, Robert's mother would stay up with her son and pray with him fervently, beseeching Jesus and God to protect Robert and their home. On some level, these prayer sessions were nice for Robert; he felt his mother's love and concern. But they did nothing to alleviate his persistent nocturnal fears. The recurring prayer sessions—and his mother's strong Christian worldview, which entailed a belief in the very real existence of demons—only served to deepen, expand, and solidify his fears. After all, when a mother confirms that there are indeed demons trying to get you, what seven-year-old on the planet would have the ability to think, know, or believe otherwise?

And it is important to understand that Robert's mother wasn't just his mother. She was also the leading exorcist in her town. She was a sort of spiritual superhero: one minute, she was a mild-mannered housewife, the next minute: Warrior for God. From the time that Robert was an infant, and throughout his childhood, his mom would get calls almost every day asking her to cast out demons from some poor afflicted soul.

She kind of became a specialist in that. Different counselors and pastors referred their possessed parishioners to her. So they would come over sometimes, or sometimes she would go. I remember going with her. One of the places was an evangelical counseling agency on Clark Street and Hilldale. It was just like a strip mall deal, but she'd go in there and do exorcisms. . . . When this stuff happened, it was as early as I can remember—I was four, five, six.

What did you think of all this, being so young?

From my perspective: fear. So she would leave and it was like Batman being called. I mean she's freaking out, she's speaking in tongues while we're driving down there, so she's "mumm mummell mummell"—just going off and then she would explain some things to me and how serious this was—just talking about the demons. She said there was the Demon of Adultery, the Demon of Pornography, and the Demon of—and she would list the demons and begin a sort of plan of attack relative to those demons—and discuss this with me. So I'm just scared shitless. I mean, I'm thinking: "This is it, like, they might get me. What if one gets loose?" I was just petrified—petrified—thinking: "what if this goes sour?" . . . The ones at the counseling center I don't have vivid memories of. The ones at home I do, you know, being in another room and hearing her and sometimes another friend or two from the church just speaking loudly in tongues and then yelling and it escalated until the point of the expulsion of the demon—or whatever.

What were they yelling?

Oh, just: "In the name of Jesus!"—the rhetoric is sort of an interesting script in and of itself: "I'm binding these demons, I'm loosing these demons and covering you in the blood of Jesus Christ!" and then speaking directly to the demons. And they would lay hands on them, anoint with oil and these types of things.

Is the person with the demons uttering any sounds?

Sometimes, yeah. There would be like the weird guttural stuff. Swearing sometimes. I remember hearing them swearing that way. That's where I learned swear words [laughs].

Robert is now 32 years old. He's a nice looking man, with engaging eyes, dark hair, pierced ears, and lots of tattoos adorning his arms. He has a real charisma about him—a quirky mix of youthful nervousness and philosophical intelligence. I met him about six or seven years ago, when I was teaching a graduate seminar on the sociology of religion, and he was one of the star students. One of the books we read that semester was about exorcisms in contemporary American Christian culture, and when it was time to discuss the book in class, Robert said that he knew many of the people in the book, that he himself had witnessed countless exorcisms, and that although he was no longer a believer, he could personally relate very deeply to the book's contents.[1] As I began thinking about writing a book on people who were once religious but are no longer, I remembered Robert and got in touch, and he was more than happy to come over to my house one Sunday night to do an interview. When we were done, I asked him if there was anyone else he knew that I might be able to interview. He recommended one of his younger brothers, Ed.

Ed is fairer than Robert, with brighter, more intense eyes. He has just about the same number of tattoos on his arms as Robert and a similarly energetic manner. He is now 28 years old.

Here's what Ed recalled when I asked him about his mother's exorcisms:

> I went to an exorcism with my mom and my little brother. We were told to wait upstairs, but we knew why we were going there. And we heard the screaming. My mom believes in them and believed that she was going to exorcise this demon out of a teenage girl at the pastor's house. . . . I remember it got so bad and one of the pastor's children was there as well, so my little brother and I and the pastor's son left the house because it was too much . . . all kinds of screaming, cusswords, you know . . . yeah, pretty weird.

For many Americans, religion is important but it is not necessarily the most important thing in their lives. But for Robert and Ed and their family, religion was everything. Though their mother was a stay-at-home mom, taking care of Robert, Ed, and two additional younger brothers, she was also a very busy exorcist. Their father was a nurse at the nearby hospital, and he held all kinds of leadership positions at church. They were a content middle-class American family, living in the suburbs. And the Bible and Jesus were never far from their ears and eyes and hearts and minds. They went to their nondenominational church frequently: once or twice on Sundays, and two or three times during the week. They prayed at home a lot: at mealtimes, before bedtime, or whenever something came up that required it. Robert and Ed's mother was more or less consumed by her Christianity. As Ed explained to me:

> *My mom's religious life—it involved a lot of time on the phone with her friends, praying. This was before the Internet and cell phones and stuff. They would get on three-way and call another person for three-way and they'd have these sort of conference calls where they would just pray for an hour or two or something as I did my schoolwork.*

This was a daily thing?

> *Yeah, a daily thing. Then I would say . . . every night a similar thing, if it wasn't just her on the phone with one person, it was many people after we'd go to bed, but we could always kind of hear her. I would say maybe once or twice a week they would pray in tongues at night and so I would hear my mom speaking some sort of gibberish to her friends that seemed super important somehow . . . you know, all the generalities of "Christianese"—just stuff about how God's working, that "God would always take care of it if we just pray more . . . it's in God's hands and God will take care of it and He always has before and He always will."*

Their mother's passion for the Lord rubbed off on the kids. Ed remembers how he often tried to convert other children in the neighborhood to his fundamentalist brand of Christianity. Sometimes he was successful, and he can still rattle off the names of various people from his old neighborhood whose families became regular churchgoers because he got their kids into it. However, other times he wasn't so successful at winning converts, which was troubling:

I worried....I would cry to my mom and—just being so broken over the fact
that I had such a close friend and I might not see them when I die, you know,
that they're not going to be going to heaven, they're living in sin...it killed me.

Robert and Ed were mostly home-schooled, because their parents didn't want them influenced by secular society. After all,
they might be taught about evolution, which was a lie. What they
needed to know was the truth: that Jesus had died for our sins
and that the Bible is the word of God. Oh, and that the apoca-
lypse was coming any day now. For Robert, the End Times were
always just around the corner:

There is one dominant thought and fear I had growing up: the end of the world
was near, and my mother was very explicit about that and very rational about
it....I remember even asking, am I going to get to go to high school? And the
answer was very clear: probably not.

Because the world would...?

Would end....There would be the millennial reign of Christ...trials and
tribulations and then the millennial reign of Christ and the saints would go to
heaven. So we were going to live through it all...the world—it was going to
hell in a hand-basket.

Throughout his junior high years, while Robert was expecting the
world to end any day, he simultaneously got heavily involved in
church youth groups. He was often tapped to serve as a youth
leader, which he did with earnest devotion. He would regularly
lead prayer sessions, witness to other kids, and attend occasional
mass exorcisms where he would join with others in laying his
hands on people, casting out demons in the name of Jesus Christ.
He recalled one particular mass exorcism that he attended in his
teens:

In Fresno...they did a mass exorcism—I mean mass. Up in front the rock band
is just jammin' and they would all of a sudden segue into some guy, and he's like

talking about all this—especially sexual stuff, like: "How many of you are masturbators? How many of you have ever...?" He was like, "This is a spiritual affliction and you're all being plagued by demonic powers!" and the worship band is kinda jammin' along, kind of working up...

How many people were in attendance?

A thousand, I don't know. It was a big group, about 80% teenagers or preteens and then a bunch of ministers or whatever—youth ministers of the different groups. I remember an ocean of people in front of me on the ground, just flopping around. I mean, flopping around, swearing.... There were the people that were being held down—whatever—the people with the oil anointing them, people just rocking...I remember...At that time I thought it was crazy, but there's something about it I still thought was real. It was weird and whatever, but...just seeing that many people, a thousand-plus people all going along with this and the insanity of it.... There were a few pivotal years where I would say I believed it and—yeah, I thought something was going on and, you know, I was sort of enamored with...like this is just this power that you have over the universe and like—you're God's conduits with this energy, this power, and, man, it's really cool, you know.

Ed was also involved in Christian youth groups as well as Christian summer camps. He was a strong believer and he had his share of powerful religious experiences:

I mean, I was wholeheartedly into it...and I went to camps.... Most of my religious experiences came through worship and I played guitar and stuff like that. I played in worship bands and we'd go to camp and I was really moved by the music more than the sermons or any words, you know. I remember—the truth—thinking "I felt God's presence here" and whatever I was feeling I definitely attributed it to something—God, the God of the Bible, the God that I believed in at the time. Yeah, absolutely.

This was in the 1980s. While most American teenagers at that time were obsessing over MTV, or new video games, or perhaps the films of John Hughes—for many others, that is, Christian teenagers such as Robert and Ed, their obsessions centered around God, Jesus, demons, heaven, hell, and the like. And people who believe in such things are still remarkably abundant. A 2008 poll revealed that 75% of Americans believe in miracles, 75% believe in the existence of heaven, 71% believe that Jesus is the son of God, 61% believe that Jesus was born of a virgin, 59% believe in the existence of the Devil, 31% believe in the existence of witches, and 71% believe in the existence of angels. Another survey, from 2005, found that 55% of Americans believe "absolutely" in Satan and another 17.6% think he "probably" exists, 43.6% are absolutely certain that demons exist and another 22.6% believe that they probably exist, and 61% are absolutely certain about the existence of angels with another 19% believing that they, too, probably exist. The members of Robert and Ed's family were among the approximately 60% or 70% of Americans who believe in angels.[2]

As Ed recalled:

Yeah, they were all in the house. "You can't see them, but there's angels in the house"—just like you and I are in this room. "They're here and they're watching over us."

But despite the protection of those ever-present angels, Robert and Ed were taught to always be on guard, for there are also demons lurking everywhere—demons that possess and afflict people, causing them personal, emotional, or physical harm. While many Christians perhaps accept the notion of Satan as some sort of abstract or metaphorical "wicked force" in the world, for Robert and Ed, there was nothing abstract or metaphorical about the Red, Horned One. Satan was real—as real as Robert and Ed themselves. One could become possessed by demons as easily as one could catch the flu. So, while most of the other kids in his neighborhood were focused on the mundane matters that are typically pondered by teenagers, young Robert was worrying about his soul's eternal salvation, thanking Jesus for shedding his atoning sacrifice, and studying the Bible. And, of course, working hard to resist the Devil and avoiding anything that would damn his soul to hell. It was all pretty scary. As Robert recalled:

> *I had such anxiety. . . . I always feared for my own salvation. I always secretly thought I would go to hell. I just kind of thought I would. I knew I wasn't quite cutting the mustard . . . so I feared hell to the point of having daily nightmares growing up, and the end of the world all tied in. The world's going to end and somehow I was going to be on the wrong side.*

One thing that could definitely land a lad like Robert on the wrong side was engaging in sinful behavior—mainly sex. His parents were very worried about this, so they became very proactive in doing all they could to make sure that Robert remained a virgin until marriage. They bought him several books released by James Dobson's conservative Christian group, Focus on the Family, that explained sex, or rather, explained *abstinence* from sex. And just to be extra safe, his parents had him go through a religious "commitment ceremony," wherein he swore to never have sex until marriage. He signed a certificate stating that he understood what a serious sin premarital sex was and how he was going to wait until he was rightfully wed and then they took him into the city and bought him a 14-karat gold promise ring, which he was to wear at all times as a symbol of his pledge to himself, to his parents, to God, and to his future wife.

> *I was pledging this to my future wife and I understand that—this is the best part—I understand that, you know, if I violate this I'm violating her, so I'm violating my future wife-to-be. That—and the going to hell—but that was the one that really stuck with me. It made sense in some way, like, "Well, I don't want to violate her," like, "I want to have a wife who I respect and respects me and I don't want to violate her." . . . . So I got this crazy-ass ring . . . the irony of ironies is that I start having sex around 15 or whatever, right, and . . . that same year the ring broke.*

Robert's loss of virginity was an emotionally wrenching experience.

The first time I had sex, I cried afterwards ... not in front of my girlfriend, but I was a little bit shaken and I left. ... Yeah, I felt horrible—"What have I done?" I had ... this like ring on my hand. It was a whole ceremony, too. We went to the jewelry district in Sacramento and picked it out, you know, my dad reads this whole thing and mom reads this whole thing. ... I'm committing my life to virginity until marriage and all that. ... So then I remember I kind of laid there and just felt like sick to my stomach, like what did I do? I fucked up! I remember thinking about: what am I going to tell my wife? That was one of the first things that popped into my head ... and I remember that night—crying and just crying and crying. ... I mean, the guilt and shame is what seems so tragic to me and the thing I'm most resentful of. I mean, it was crippling.

Although Robert had doubts and periodic bouts of skepticism about his religion, and although his church attendance had become sporadic later in his teens, he still remained a Christian and, with some pressure from his mother, enrolled in seminary at a fundamentalist, conservative Bible college at age 19. He went on to earn a master's degree in philosophy, religion, and ethics. He was one of the best students in his cohort, and his professors asked him to help write various position papers and pamphlets on things like Christian apologetics and opposition to gay marriage. He was on the path to becoming a pastor.

But it didn't happen.

Today, Robert is no longer a Christian. He doesn't believe in God. He doesn't think the Bible is divine. He doesn't worry about his soul's eternal salvation or damnation. He no longer dwells in a demon-haunted world. I asked him how he would describe himself now:

I'm definitely not a supernaturalist in any way. ... I'm a humanist, to be sure ... it's like, I don't know how to classify myself other than just saying "religiously unmusical."

Robert's younger brother, Ed, has also lost his fundamentalist faith. He doesn't go to church anymore, doesn't pray, and doesn't believe that the Bible is the Word of God. Does he at least still consider himself a Christian?

No, no. Definitely not.

What would you say you are, then?

I don't know....I'm open to the idea that there's something out there, you know? But I look at the world and if I try to think of what that "thing" that's out there might be like ...I mean, I have such a hard time saying I could have any knowledge about whatever might be out there ...I don't know. That's the whole thing: we can't know....I just take more of a humanistic approach to life now.... I've taken God out of it now and feel better about myself for doing things that way.

* * *

How did this happen? How did two boys raised in a Christian fundamentalist home—boys who had so strongly believed what they had been taught to believe—lose their faith and reject their religion? Why is it that Robert, who once believed in demons and angels, no longer subscribes to supernatural beliefs and has become irreligious? Why is it that Ed, who used to convert neighborhood kids to Christianity and who regularly felt the peaceful presence of God, now embraces a decidedly agnostic view?

Robert and Ed's journey away from religion is quite rare. Most people accept the religious beliefs that they were taught as children, are sustained by those beliefs throughout their lives, and pass those beliefs on to their children and grandchildren. But, much to their mother's anguish, Robert and Ed didn't follow this typical trajectory.

For Robert, the journey to secularity took place over the course of many years. There was no specific "faith-shattering moment," no bearded, secular professor who challenged his religious beliefs with piercing acumen, no irreligious girlfriend who convinced him that it was all bullshit. He didn't read a specific book that planted seeds of skeptical doubt. Although he did eventually go on to read books critical of Christianity by such skeptics as Bertrand Russell and Richard Dawkins, he came to these works well after his withdrawal from faithful Christianity. His mother's overbearing religious zealotry was probably one of the more powerful forces that lead him to irreligion, yet while Robert rejected the religion of his mother, he never rejected her, and they have a good relationship to this day. I asked Robert directly if he thought that perhaps his rejection of Christianity could be explained as a sort of a rebellion against his exorcist mother.

> *Yeah, I mean, I would—at some level—I grant part of it. But I think that other than the issues with my mother, I had rational, relational, social issues with religious teaching and doctrine in the church. Doctrine, I think, is the most important part. Because ... it was really that I truly did not believe the things that I was supposed to believe.*

Robert describes his letting go of religion as a life-long journey, and when he reflects back on it now, he likens his secularity to homosexuality: he thinks that perhaps it was always there, deep inside him even as a child, and that although he tried his best to ignore it and repress it—and perhaps didn't even always fully understand it—as a grown man he could no longer deny it. He gave Christianity his best shot. But in the end, it just wasn't for him. One of his earliest memories of suppressed skepticism is when he first spoke in tongues as a child:

> *I remember there was a lot of pressure—I couldn't have been more than four or five, maybe six—to speak in tongues. Because I hadn't started yet, or whatever. I remember just feeling this guilt and shame that I hadn't done it and was I just kind of waiting for it to happen ... ? Until we went to one of these conventions, and ... I remember ... I just picked it up on cue and started doing it. ...*

Are you believing it at this time? Or are you kind of just doing—I mean when you spoke in tongues, did you think that, yeah, the spirit took?

No—that's the thing. It's so weird to say it, but I remember even feeling guilty for kind of faking it. But, you know, it was like the Emperor's New Clothes for me: everyone's doing it and I felt like I had to do it, otherwise I would continue to stick out. I . . . felt this pressure—like I was failing. I wasn't spiritual enough or whatever, so I just kind of went for it.

Looking back now, Robert compares his religiousness to a roller-coaster, going up and down from faithful acceptance to skeptical inquiry.

I mean, I think I've always been fairly inquisitive and so when I was told about the End Times—I mean, when I was seven, eight, nine years old, I remember asking very pointed and very critical questions sometimes of my parents. . . . I always asked these questions. I remember being fairly dissatisfied with most of the answers.

What were some of the questions?

I read the Bible at a fairly early age . . . and had questions based on that. So reading the Old Testament . . . and, "What about this? It says there's capital crimes for adultery and these things." I remember being fairly struck with the barbarism and that sort of thing, and it just seemed so crazy. I remember my mom just really explained it to me as "It was the way things were back then." It just didn't seem to make sense. So all this stuff was swimming around and I began to obsess over it, probably in junior high, and I remember having my first very serious doubts and saying this whole package seems screwy.

When Robert would find himself seriously doubting this or that religious teaching, the result would be guilt and shame. So he tried his best to stay faithful—to just keep on believing and to push the doubts away as best he could. But at age 15, he told his parents that he didn't want to go to church anymore.

Mainly, I said I just can't take it. People are just, I don't know, ridiculous. And the youth pastor really was a total chump. Actually, he ended up having an affair with someone. . . . Except for one youth pastor, virtually all the religious leaders that I grew up with got involved with some sort of scandal—sexual, money...they're all charlatans.

Did you believe in God throughout high school? Or did you just kind of...

I don't know. I mean I think for reasons mainly of some deep-seated fear, I would say, "I believe in Jesus." I would have probably said that. I don't think I ever told anyone I was atheist or something. But pretty close.... I went back and forth, and I would kind of take a stab at trying to reinforce religious beliefs.... I was struggling with it and trying to make sense of it, but I pretty much left it in my high school years.

By his late teens, Robert's mother was truly worried about her son's spiritual fate.

I remember my mother just crying and crying over my soul, basically, during this period.

Robert had his heart set on going to UC Berkeley, but, to appease his distressed mother, he agreed to at least check out a bible college and to meet with some of the administrators and professors there. He found them extremely nice and thoughtful. And he was impressed—they seemed scholarly, intellectual, engaging. He applied, was accepted, and although he was candid about some of his questions and doubts, the school simply placed him on "spiritual probation," which meant that he had to meet with someone from the college once a month to discuss and work on his faith.

Were you an atheist at this point, just going through the motions of being a good Christian college student? Or did you still believe?

I'd say, yeah, in the middle of the year I would say I believed. I even wrote some articles for this conservative Christian think tank. That's what kind of broke me, because I did a couple—like on these doctrinal issues and one on

God's omnipotence and the limits of that. I wrote some pieces on the problem of evil. I really got into that. Then they asked me to write one on homosexuality. There was this kind of crisis around that because one of my really good friends was gay and that was always an issue I just avoided, and then they wanted me to do this—write this piece. I know I wrote some of it—that was the last piece that I did with them. I don't think that I finished it.

They wanted you to take a . . . ?

Yeah, a biblical position against homosexuality.

Okay, and so you're writing this . . .

And I had this crisis of conscience. And I was like: I don't believe this shit. I don't think homosexuality is an abomination. . . . So I wrote part of it—but I didn't finish it . . . and that ended it.

So do you know when you finally realized that you weren't a Christian believer?

Yeah, that next year.

What happened?

Umm . . . I kind of just stewed over the things that I had kind of thought—I sort of saw through the Christian apologetic stuff, the rationalism stuff, and realized I really just wasn't convinced by those arguments. I gave it a shot . . . and I guess I just didn't believe it.

I also asked Ed how he accounts for his loss of faith. One influential factor was obviously his older brother, Robert. As Ed was going through his teenage years, he knew that Robert's skepticism was sharpening. They often had conversations about inconsistencies within Christianity, certain things that just didn't make rational, logical sense. Ed loved and respected Robert, and his big brother's weakening faith had a definite impact on him.

Then Ed had a similar experience with one of his good friends, who was also a Christian but was starting to question his faith.

> *There was one very close friend in high school, probably freshman year. We were tossing around these ideas of—we started wrestling with these ideas— difficult things, you know. Like: where do angels come from? Are they good? If … God knows everything we're going to do before we do it, then do we have any choice not to, you know? All that kind of stuff. … I'm asking questions that I never thought of and it's getting harder and harder to get answers.*

What were some of the questions?

> *Like … evolution versus creation. Science says carbon dating and this and then—I always interpreted the Bible literally as a child, and now I'm looking into this. Is it just analogous to a creation story or is it literal? So all this stuff … and I started realizing that all the stuff I was getting taught … I started seeing through the things I was being taught and it wasn't sitting right. … So I think, like, faith was falling away … .*

When Ed went off to college, one of his roommates had been raised in a home similar to his, with the same general religious outlook. The two of them spent many nights talking about what they had been taught to believe as children and about how they just didn't buy it anymore. They found other students like them— young men and women who had been raised Christian but now thought it was all baloney. To "prove" their apostasy to themselves and to one another, they began publicly denying the Holy Spirit. In the New Testament, one finds the following declaration: "Whoever blasphemes against the Holy Spirit will never be forgiven; he is guilty of an eternal sin" (Mark 3:29). This is frequently interpreted by Christian fundamentalists to mean that while God can and will forgive any and every sin, the one thing that is unforgivable in the eyes of the Lord is the blaspheming of the Holy Spirit. Once you do that, you're sunk. You're going to hell, no matter what. So, in order to bolster their atheist mettle and to "prove" that they were no longer believers—that they were true "ex-tians" (ex-Christians)—Ed and his friends in college would engage in this atheist ritual.[3]

Just denying the Holy Spirit, you know: "I deny it—and if that means I can't go to heaven, then I want to seal it now so that it's done." Like a lot of anger came out.

So there was a period where you were kind of angry?

Absolutely.

And what were you angry about?

I feel like I was lied to. I feel like I was too young to be making decisions that I feel like were made for me. I was mad at my parents, really mad at my mom for keeping me from—who knows how different I would be today or who knows what path I would have gone down? I was just pretty pissed.... I was like, "I've been taken," you know? Just childhood—you know—like, I was home-schooled, which was big. I never went to school. I had no elementary experiences, no teachers that impacted my life until I was almost a teenager. Yeah, just being a kid, you know what I mean? And being carefree. Life was always pretty serious. God takes you very seriously and your actions. That's a lot for a kid to bear, a lot of stress. I still bite my nails.... It was almost too much to bear, you know? Somehow I definitely feel victimized.

Do you plan on having kids some day?

Absolutely. I just got engaged last week.

Oh, congratulations.... Is your wife religious?

No, she grew up in Vermont—like—a tiny little town and we met in college. She had been to one Catholic mass in her freshman year of college and had never been to any other church service. She didn't know who Noah was. She doesn't know the creation story. I mean she's heard roughly of Adam and Eve, but she wouldn't have known the tree they ate from, she wouldn't have known what creature gave them the apple, if it was an apple. And I loved it, you know what I mean? I just like—it was so cool just that she didn't even know.

So when you have your kids, and they come home from school one day and they say, "Do you believe there's a God?" What would you say?

I would say maybe, you know: "Not any God that's been written about." That's what I'd say, you know. Sally and I have said that we won't take the kids to church. If they wanted to go to church, we'd let them go with their friends. It's not going to be this "religion is evil" kind of thing. . . . I think there's a value to having a reverence for something bigger than yourself, you know: "There's something out there." Sure, you know what I mean? It kind of helps you put things into perspective. "It's not all about me." You know what I mean? Whether I have to say it's something bigger than me I'm not sure, but I think those are good values to have. But we won't take them to church. If they think there's a God and they want to start investigating that, I might even help them, you know. I'd say, "These are people's quests. People have thought this throughout humanity and the fact that you're thinking this is only natural."

Ed is now halfway through law school. He wants to go into the field of criminal justice and defend the wrongly accused. Robert is currently a very popular and well-respected professor of philosophy at a community college. He is married to a beautiful, bright woman who teaches French and they just bought a charming, wooden-floored house in a really nice neighborhood. Is everything perfect for Robert and Ed? I doubt it—everyone has problems. But from my limited perspective, they seem to be doing very well.

*   *   *

There is something remarkable about people who were raised in extremely religious homes, who adopted and internalized the beliefs impressed upon them by their parents, only to shed those beliefs later in life. There is something fascinating about people who can believe that there is a God—believe it with all their heart and all their soul—and then, one day, no longer hold that core, central belief. For some, this transition from religiosity to secularity might be viewed as a deep loss, the loss of the most important, sustaining, affirming thing they have. Yet for some people, it simply can't be helped. Secularity happens. For such people, their own personal rejection of religion is a loss that is dwarfed by what is gained, which is something positive, freeing, and rewarding. In the words of the French philosopher and believing-Catholic-turned-atheist André Comte-Sponville:

> It felt like a liberation—everything suddenly seemed simpler, lighter, stronger and more open. It was as if I had left childhood behind me, with its fantasies and fears, its closeness and languorousness, and entered the real world at long last—the adult world, the world of action, the world of truth, unhampered by forgiveness or Providence. Such responsibility! Such joy! Yes, I am convinced that my life has been better—more lucid, freer and more intense—since I became an atheist.[4]

2

⚬⚬

Stopped Making Sense

David is 58 years old. He was born and raised in rural Ghana. Once a devout, faithful, and passionately active Jehovah's Witness, he has left the faith. About two years ago, he emailed me, after reading one of my books. We exchanged a few messages back and forth, discussing religion, atheism, and other topics. He had a lot to say, and his emails conveyed a notable degree of vim. So when I told him that I was working on a new book about apostasy, he was more than willing to get together for an interview.

Then, of course, I got into Noah's story. I broke it down where it's not possible for an old man, 600-year-old man, and his wife and his children, who are probably 500 years old, to go and build a structure the size of the Colosseum just so God could bring all these animals in and save them from a flood. . . . Well, I was becoming very radical—very, very critical. And I decided . . . the Bible cannot be true. Noah's ark? Eight people could not have built a structure that size and to get all these animals and bring them in . . . it's not possible. You could not have a giraffe from East Africa go across East Africa to the North and go to Iraq and get into an ark. . . .

So what is faith? Faith is believing in something that you don't know anything about and yet you believe it happened. Well . . . faith is like idolatry.

You're just believing just because you want to believe. But if you're going to
believe something that is going to affect our lives, we should have evidence
to support it. . . . So faith must be based on evidence, and if you can't give me
the evidence, I cannot believe in it. I'll say, "Show me the evidence and I'll
believe it."

To some readers, David may seem cold or disgruntled. To others, perhaps he comes off as rational and enlightened. Either way, what I wanted to capture here was the fact that, for David as well as for many other apostates, at some point in the recounting of the story of why someone rejected religion, he or she will emphasize a personal loss of belief—a difficulty accepting that certain specifics of the religion that were once considered to be true. People will stress that an integral part of their apostasy is simply a matter of their coming to regard certain religious beliefs as false. For David, it was the story of Noah's ark. He once believed it as a genuine, factual account of a significant historical event. Now, he sees it as mythological nonsense.

Colleen is 21 years old and works as a receptionist in a law firm. Although she was immersed in religion for much of her life, today she considers herself an "atheist" or "agnostic," depending on her mood. For Colleen, like David, key biblical stories became increasingly hard to swallow:

I went to my uncle and asked him, "Do we believe the story of Adam and Eve?"
He said, "Why do you ask?" I remember thinking: well, if we all come from
Adam and Eve, a man and a woman, they did it, they had kids . . . well, how
did those kids have kids? So if the whole entire world is based off of between
one man and one woman, the only way that they could populate was by
brothers and sisters having sex with each other, or with their mom and dad,
so it would be incest. So I don't see how an entire human race can be popu-
lated out of two people. We would be deformed. That doesn't make sense. And
he told me, "We believe everything that's in the Bible." I remember thinking:
well, that just does not make sense because there's no way that I'm a result of
incestual relations like—but—that just doesn't make sense. So I just kind of
shook it off—like—"this is stupid."

For Max, it was the whole concept of "sin." Max is 65 years old. He grew up in Colorado, and today he lives in Texas. He is a retired Army dentist. He was raised in a churchgoing, pray-at-mealtimes Lutheran family. He believed in the stories he was taught in Sunday school and at Bible camp, but by his early teens he was skeptical, and today he is an atheist.

> *The point that I recall...was without any hesitation whatsoever...was the light bulb moment in my life. I remember in my early teens, I was say 13 or 14, and I was in vacation Bible school in the summertime, probably in June. There was this nice young lay teacher who was teaching us our lessons and kind of in the middle of one of these lessons she said, "By the way, you were born in sin." I said, wait a minute. When I was born I couldn't see, I couldn't hear, I couldn't think, I couldn't talk, I couldn't do anything but pee, poop, and suck on my mother's breast and you're telling me I was born in sin? We got a problem here. That was the end of my faith at that point.... This has got to be rational and logical and I can't believe that someone would—I may have been to church sometimes after that with the family and subsequently at weddings and funerals—but I never believed after that.*

Apostasy often occurs when certain key religious beliefs, tenets, teachings, stories, creeds, or articles of faith simply stop making sense. I'm tempted to call it "acquired incredulity syndrome." For certain individuals, it was the recognition that the findings of modern science—from astronomy to geology, from genetics to evolution, and from physics to archaeology—flatly contradicted so many of the central claims of the Bible, that it rendered them manifestly unbelievable.[1]

For other apostates, it isn't so much that their religion stops making sense in the light of scientific discovery, but rather, that it stops making sense in the light of their own moral reasoning. The problem becomes the perceived immorality of God. In this vein of emergent incredulity, it isn't that some religious claim or event in history doesn't make scientific sense—such as Noah's ark, the resurrection, or the Virgin Birth. Rather, it is God's apparent lack of righteousness that is the problem.

Recall Robert, son of the exorcist mother. His parents taught him that only people who believed as they did— nondenominational, Evangelical Christians who were "saved" and had a personal relationship with Jesus Christ—would go to heaven. The rest of humanity would go to hell—by God's decree. For Robert, this was manifestly immoral:

> *I couldn't believe—and didn't believe—that all of my friends were going to hell or that that could be reconciled with any notion of a good God. I remember being nine, ten years old—it just wrecked me. I just ... said, "It doesn't make sense, Mom." Especially my Mormon friend ... he was just a good person. Someone I really wanted to be like. I thought he was just morally—and all the above—just a fun guy. And his family was great. So I thought that just doesn't make sense to me, like, I couldn't come to terms with that being God's master plan. Yeah, my neighbor two doors up who was a Jew. ... It just didn't seem to make sense.*

Many apostates have a very difficult time sustaining belief in a God that they at some point come to view as immoral. They read passages in the Bible wherein God wantonly kills children, or commands his followers to commit genocide or systematic rape. They read passages in the Qu'ran where God is murderous, blood-thirsty, and downright wicked. They read passages in the Book of Mormon where God is manifestly racist, or in Doctrines and Covenants, where God is shockingly sexist. Such scriptural knowledge is hard to reconcile with a deity they want to conceive of as being wholly good.[2]

Ivan, age 33, is a former Methodist who now considers himself an atheist. As he explained,

> *You know, you think about it and then you start to think about what are these records I have of God, and you think about the Old Testament and about how God pretty much asked for genocide on several occasions. ... As you become a little more comfortable questioning these things that you were so confident about, you get to the "a-ha" moment. Like, alright, I got it. It's not really what I'm supposed to believe.*

If it isn't God's actions that turn people off, it is simply the state of the world, which is rife with pain and injustice. Many people find their belief in God hard to reconcile with the suffering that permeates the world. Such was Rose's experience. She is 54 years old, grew up in Georgia, and has worked as a doctor for many years. The suffering that Rose has seen over the course of her medical career has definitely been detrimental to her belief in God:

> I work in a hospital. I see a lot of people die. Um [long pause, heavy sigh]... I think it sometimes makes me question—when I see somebody go through a painful death. What's the point here? And I think if anything it would make me feel—um—that there is no Higher Being looking over us, trying to make things better. Because some people have really bad deaths.

Bagrat is a former Muslim of Persian descent. Although Bagrat always identified as a Muslim while growing up—reading and studying the Qu'ran, praying five times daily, and believing that Muhammad was God's true messenger—today, as a law student at the University of Nebraska, he is a convinced atheist. At the root of his loss of faith was his inability to square his ideal of God with the reality of the gross suffering in the world:

> Why did your grandma, who is 95 years old, deserve to live even though she has six different ailments and doctors finally saved her again, but a 60-year-old woman dies? She doesn't deserve to live? A father of nine children that are already on welfare, he passes away. Let's say he was a good father and he would actually raise some good kids... why did he die? God's okay with a poor Indian girl being born to be a prostitute in India and— from the time that she's two years old—she's sold for her body until the time she dies? Who's your God, then? Why didn't he step in then? It's questions like that that make me realize we're here in one of two situations— which is honestly frightening for me—if we're in the first. The first: there is a God and he just really sucks. He's a terrible God. He's actually pretty lazy. He doesn't like to be pro-active.... So that leads me to the second possibility: that maybe one just doesn't exist... If I were gonna believe in a

God, I wanna believe that he's a good God, and I want observations to reflect that. But they don't.

Bagrat is clearly not the only one to find it difficult to make sense of a God who seems indifferent to human misery or is powerless to alleviate it. Many apostates say this was central to their rejection of theism. And such feelings of moral indignation have haunted the hearts and minds of humanity for centuries. Perhaps the first person to articulate as much was the Greek philosopher Epicurus (341 BCE–270 BCE), who stated the following more than 2,000 years ago:

> Either God wants to get rid of evil, but he can't; or God can, but he doesn't want to; or God neither wants to nor can, or he both wants to and can. If God wants to, but can't, then he's not all-powerful. If he can, but doesn't want to, he's not all-loving. If he neither can nor wants to, he's neither all-powerful nor all-loving. And if he wants to and can— then why doesn't he remove the evils?[3]

A common belief in the United States, and one that gets voiced in the media on a regular basis, is that people who don't believe in God are immoral. This may be one of the reasons that surveys report wide distrust and dislike of atheists. And yet, the notion that nonreligious people are immoral is simply untrue. Throughout my conversations with apostates, it became clear that they maintained a heightened sense of ethics, expressing a passionate desire for moral order. They desperately want a world characterized by fairness, justice, respect, compassion, and love. And they simply cannot stomach, let alone excuse, a God that does not seem to share their moral orientation. Why does God create or allow earthquakes and tsunamis that kill hundreds of thousands of people? Why does God send people who don't worship him to hell? Why did God allow the Nazis, the Khmer Rouge, and the Hutus to slaughter millions of innocent people? For most people—and certainly most religious people—the answer is that we simply can't know. God's ways are not our ways, and while they are inscrutable to us now, they will be made known to us, in time. As the Christian philosopher William Lane Craig has argued, our comprehension of God is limited, so "actions that appear disastrous in the short term may redound to the greatest good" and moral evils we witness or experience here on earth "may be justified only in light of eternity."[4]

For a handful of people, many who become apostates, that line of thinking just doesn't cut it.

*   *   *

To say that apostates often come to see previously accepted religious teachings as false, implausible, or nonsensical is important, because many apostates consider it to be a central ingredient of their apostasy. But how does it happen, exactly? What causes men and women to reject beliefs they once defended, to abandon beliefs they once found comfort in, to question the previously unquestionable?

It is one thing to be secular if you've been raised secular. In such cases, an individual's lack of faith or disinterest in religion can readily be accounted for as a result of his or her upbringing and childhood socialization. But what about people who were raised in religious homes and were socialized to be religious from an early age? What about people for whom—at least at some point in their lives—faith was deeply important, religious rituals had sacred meaning, and theological beliefs were existentially essential? How do such people shed those beliefs, exactly? What are some of the specific factors or personal experiences that trigger their acquired incredulity? What causes them to eventually come to the conclusion that their religion doesn't make sense?

3

❧

Misfortune

David, the former Jehovah's Witness from Ghana, whose skeptical musings about Noah's ark led him to apostasy, sat in my backyard on a sunny Sunday. His face was animated as he conveyed his personal story; one minute he is joyful, and the next, quite serious. He appeared to relish the opportunity to explain his "escape" from religion, an escape he sees as perhaps the most profound, most pivotal development in his life. But it didn't actually start with Noah's ark. It started with some unfortunate events in his life.

Here's how David tells the story:

I ended up moving to Northern California. I got a job. And with my pay-check—with what was left—I couldn't pay my rent. My electricity was turned off ... the phone had been cut off. It was during this time—I came home, I just sat down and asked myself: Well, as a Jehovah's Witness, I did everything I was supposed to do. Dedicated my life. Got baptized. I believe in Jehovah, Jesus, field service....I never missed field service, my meetings—I never missed. I was always prepared when I have an assignment. I did so well. People always commended me on my delivery. If God is supposed to be rewarding us with everything we need—I need a wife—I prayed and this is what I got and this is where I am? I prayed and prayed and I asked the question: why does—just like Jesus did when supposedly he was on the cross and in the torture state, said—why have you forsaken me? Why didn't you hear my prayers? After I finished praying, I was in tears. I sat on the couch and said: maybe I'm asking the wrong question. Does God really answer prayers? That's when it hit me: no, he doesn't. There is no God out there listening to every individual's prayer.

Back in Ghana, David's father had been a farmer and his mother was a seamstress. They lived in a rural village about two hours outside of Accra. David's parents were active leaders in their local religious community. He remembers spending many hours, weeks, months, and years—along with his parents and siblings— going door to door, trying to win converts, as is the hallmark of the Jehovah's Witness tradition. As he got older, his involvement with the Witnesses only grew deeper. He was a committed, true believer. He was also very bright and was often at the top of his class in high school. After graduating, he wanted to go to medical school and become a doctor. But the Witnesses said no. They were certain that the world was coming to an apocalyptic end in 1975, so why go to medical school? Having complete faith in their pre- diction of the world's imminent demise, David didn't go—this was a fateful decision he would regret all his life. He eventually moved to the United States and began studying computers, bid- ing his time until the world came to an end. In America, he imme- diately became immersed in his religious community, attending meetings, going to church (or what Witnesses call a "Kingdom Hall") regularly, and witnessing door to door. But he was lonely. He wanted a wife.

One of the things about Jehovah's Witnesses is you cannot marry outside of the organization. You have to marry only in the Lord and only in the Lord is a Jehovah's Witness. . . . So I was having difficulty marrying, finding somebody. Eventually, I met this lady in Phoenix and for a Jehovah's Witness, when you hear the words "Jehovah, Jesus"—it's like music to your ears. That's all I heard from this lady. And I married her. I had asked the elders before I mar- ried her, "What do you think about this sister?" "Oh, she's a beautiful sister,

she loves Jehovah and she's always out to service." Okay, sounds good to me.
I married her and found out she did not believe—well, she still believes it as
the organization, but morally she didn't believe she had to live a moral life.
Basically, she cheated on me for nine years of the marriage. She never left her
ex-boyfriend. Eventually she ended up having two kids while we're married
by another man. I was out of the country, in Saudi Arabia, working. I went to
Saudi Arabia to make money so we can get back on our feet. I came back and
she had two children. Of course, within the nine years of the adultery and all
that, it was a miserable life for me. So when I came back, she decided to file for
divorce . . . and I was hit with very heavy child support, alimony—$3,400 a
month after taxes.

David had done everything right, since the time he was a small child. He had studied his Bible diligently, prayed fervently, followed the principles of his religious denomination obediently, attended meetings and worship services happily, didn't go to medical school because the elders told him not to, married a women his elders recommended, and so on. His heart was—and had always been—deeply committed to Jehovah. He was a true servant of the Lord. And what did he get for all this? A cheating wife who went on to divorce him, a foundering professional life, and barely enough money to pay for his phone bill and electric bill and train fare to a job he couldn't have been less enthusiastic about.

It was approximately a year or so after his divorce that he found himself in that small apartment, asking himself and his God, why if he had done everything right, why was his life such a mess? If a devout life is to be a blessed life, was his life so miserable? Surely, countless men and women have been in David's shoes. There probably hasn't ever been a religious person alive who hasn't, at one time or another, wondered why things aren't going well despite their faithful commitment to their Lord. And that's certainly the reason that the Book of Job is such a perennial favorite; whoever wrote that story some 2,500 years ago clearly understood situations like David's and was familiar with the piercing doubt and skeptical questions that difficult situations are apt to generate. But most religious people don't let their unfortunate life circumstances erode their faith. They are able to come up with an explanation to make sense of their situation and thereby maintain their religious beliefs. But this was not the case for David. For him, everything started to unravel:

> That's when I started researching.... This Bible story—what is it about? And then I went to Adam and Eve.... Alright, if you are God you are all-seeing and you know everything, and you created Adam. You know his thought processes, what is going to happen. You do all that and you plant him in a garden where he was happy with his wife and he was going about. But from the heavens where you are, you see Satan headed towards them. And if you're God and you know everything, you knew exactly what he was going to do—to deceive them and turn them against you, and you know the consequence of what will happen from this disobedience. You allowed him to come and deceive them and then you punish them with death and pain and every horrible thing, diseases, and the woman will go through childbirth in pain? You allow the devil to come through? He allowed it to happen and then to blame man for being disobedient, even though this powerful creature came down and deceived them? Now you come up with a cockamamie scheme that you're going to send your son from heaven to come all the way down to die for their sins so they can be saved? This is a fairy tale. This whole Bible story is just a myth and people have to come to grips with that.

David's rejection of his religion clearly began with skeptical questions that arose in the wake of unfortunate events in his life—his wife's infidelity, their subsequent divorce, his struggle to make ends meet. He had been faithful all his life, and he had believed that this faithfulness would bear fruit. Instead, he felt forsaken. God wasn't holding up his end of the bargain. That's when the skeptical questions truly took hold, leading David to think more critically about the faith that he had subscribed to all his life, to examine it with new eyes. His conclusion was that the beliefs that he had held for so long simply didn't make sense anymore. The Bible was transformed in David's eyes from the most important of all divine revelations into a fairy tale. Because David's life had become marked by misfortune, he then wondered whether God even existed at all.

Barry had a similar story. He is 53 years old, lives in Northern California, and works as a psychologist. For most of his life, Barry was a dutiful, believing Catholic. He went through all the rituals and prescribed rites of passage of Catholicism; he believed what he was taught about Jesus, Mary, heaven, hell, and the Bible. And he definitely believed in God, to whom he prayed regularly. Today, however, he is an atheist. When I asked him what caused him to reject his religion, he spoke directly about his loss of belief in God. But this loss of belief didn't occur out of the blue. It took place during a rather traumatic period of his life.

Barry and his wife met when they were in college. They were both life-long devout Catholics, and they endeavored to do things "right," that is, they abstained from sexual intercourse until they were duly wed. They lived as a good, faithful Catholic couple for several years, but then things started to fall apart, for a variety of reasons. It was during this marital collapse that Barry found himself, at age 40, questioning his religion:

> *That was when I started thinking about it, really. . . . Almost immediately when I started to consider that, it just made sense that there was not a God. There's so much trouble in the world, there's so much that . . . I mean, I'm a scientist. I've got my degree in biology, I've got my master's degrees in information systems and in psychology, so the basis for my understanding of things is reason. I just . . . it wasn't reasonable to think that an omniscient, omnipotent power would create such a flawed universe. . . . After we broke up, one of the things I reflected on was that we did all that "right" and ended up getting divorced . . . the ultimate in failure in terms of a Catholic relationship. Of course, the church doesn't even see that, doesn't even recognize that. . . . When I looked at that— how could there be a God that says that if you do this all right, then everything's going to be okay? We do all the right things and it's still broken. That was like the pivotal moment . . . and it was like . . . and I like to use the biblical expression, it was like the scales fell from my eyes. It was like everything made so much sense when I stopped believing in God. Yeah, once I had turned the corner, it was a moment of clarity.*

Like David, Barry had done everything a faithful believer ought to do. And he had believed in all that he was supposed to believe in. And yet the marriage he entered into—under the proper religious auspices—had failed. What God had presumably joined together had been sadly torn asunder. It was his failed marriage that essentially provided the spark for his skeptical questions and doubts about God's existence. He ended up concluding that belief in God was unwarranted and illogical. It just didn't resonate any longer.

THE FAILURE OF PRAYER

On some level, prayer just sort of makes sense. It feels natural, instinctive. When we desperately want something to happen, we wish for it. When we feel scared or threatened, we automatically find ourselves strongly hoping for safety or deliverance. For many people, that's what prayer is essentially all about: beseeching God to protect us or provide us with what we need or want. As Jesus promised in Mathew 21:22, "And all things, whatsoever ye shall ask in prayer, believing, ye shall receive." Given all of this, one can understand why prayer is so ubiquitous. According to recent Gallup surveys, 29% of American adults say they "always" pray, another 22% say they pray "frequently," and an additional 34% say they pray "occasionally," which means that about 9 out of every 10 American adults pray, at least some of the time. And according to a recent study by the Pew Forum on Religion and Public Life, 58% of American adults claim to pray daily, with an additional 17% claiming to pray at least once a week. That's a lot of prayer.[1]

But what happens when prayers aren't answered? Most religious people have a slew of relatively successful ways of dealing with this inevitability. For example, they'll tell themselves that God has other, better plans for them. Or they'll say that they must not be praying hard enough or that their faith must not be pure enough. Or they'll convince themselves that God actually has answered their prayers, just not in a way that is obvious to them yet. But for some people—an interesting minority—these excuses become just that: excuses. They had faith, they prayed to God, their prayers weren't answered, and apostasy is the result.

Penny is 29 years old. She grew up in a small town near Pasadena, California, the daughter of working-class parents— her mom was a dental assistant and her dad worked for the electric company. She attended a Foursquare Gospel church with her family every Sunday morning and every Wednesday night, she went to a private Christian school for her elementary years, she spoke in tongues as a teenager, and she was a very strong believer for most of her life:

> *Everything that I had been taught was what I believed. I didn't really have much exposure to anything else, so, you know, I believed the Genesis creation story— I believed that it was literal. I believed that basically that any sort of problem I had in life I needed to pray about or read the Bible.... I definitely—I believed that Jesus was in my heart and I prayed the prayer to become saved....I believed that when I died I was going to go to heaven.*

The first crack in Penny's Christian faith appeared when she was only nine years old. It was a traumatic break, and it never healed. It festered, grew, and eventually joined up with other, subsequent cracks until her faith was completely broken. That very first crack involved her cat, Theo:

> *I remembered when I was probably eight or nine...my cat ran away. I prayed so diligently that God would return my cat—that Theo would come home. I looked through my Bible and I found this verse about if you have as much faith the size of a mustard seed, you can move mountains. I highlighted it and I prayed over it and I just believed that even if she had died that God would bring her back because God can do anything, right? And the cat never came back, and I got increasingly upset about it and would cry and cry and cry. I'm getting emotional right now talking about it.... I was so just...I guess disappointed....I'm going to cry, but [has to take a moment to regain composure]....Because I was so sure that God would answer my prayers and he didn't...I remember thinking that even if Theo's dead, God can raise Theo from the dead because, you know, Jesus*

raised Lazarus so there's a precedent there and my cat will come back....I had
counted on God and I had believed in him and in his word and I had faith and
none of it worked.

Today, Penny would classify herself as irreligious or secular. She wouldn't call herself an atheist, because she sees that designation as a little too strong. But when it comes to the Christian religion that she once so strongly believed in, she says, "I don't believe any of it any more and I don't really see the point of it."

Carol is 21 years old. Like Penny, something happened to her when she was young and her prayers also went unanswered. Carol grew up in a suburb of San Francisco. He mother was a book-keeper, and her alcoholic father wasn't around much. She regularly attended a Baptist church, was involved in their youth group, and even went on several missionary trips to Mexico when she was a teenager. As for her beliefs:

I believed it. I really believed that Jesus had come to earth and had died on the
cross for our sins so that I could go to heaven after I died. I believed that....I
believed in the power of prayer, so I prayed every night.

However, when Carol was 11, she developed severe acne. It was, for her, a devastating blight. And so, just as she had always been taught to do, she turned to God.

I prayed one of the same prayers every single night: for God to take away my
acne. I had bad acne as a child. It tortured me. I thought that God had
"blanked" me. That was one of the reasons why—well, there were a lot of
other factors—but one of the reasons why I stopped believing.

At age 11, Carol wasn't able to reject God outright. Instead, she interpreted or rationalized God's unwillingness to clear up her acne as some sort of divine punishment: perhaps she was too pretty or too vain, and God wanted to make her less pretty in order to teach her the value of humility. Like Penny, Carol didn't abandon her Christianity until a decade or so after this bout of failed prayer. But the seeds of skepticism and disappointment were planted with that experience, seeds that would eventually blossom into a full rejection of religion. Today, Carol is a convinced nonbeliever. She doesn't like to label herself as an atheist per se, because, like Penny, she finds that word too harsh, too negative. But she is one in orientation if not in self-designation.

DEATH OF A LOVED ONE

It is fascinating how bad or painful events can cause some people to feel closer to God and more committed to their religion, while other people react by rejecting God and religion. Several years ago, a close friend of mine lost his younger brother. My friend's brother was 19 years old, and he was a volunteer in the Spanish army. One night, while in his barracks, his sergeant got drunk and belligerent and pulled out his gun and shot my friend's brother in the heart. Just like that. A devastating murder. But I recall how, in the days and weeks after the murder, my friend's mother was able to find comfort in her religious faith. She was certain that her murdered son was up in heaven with God and that she would be with him again some day, for all of eternity. She did not question why God would allow her youngest child to be senselessly murdered. She knew that God was supreme and benevolent, and she trusted in him completely, even in the face of such a tragedy. About a year after this happened, I was teaching a night class at a community college. One of my students, a young woman, told me that her 18-year-old brother had recently been killed by a drunk driver. At the time of the accident, he was engaged and was about to start college. The student told me that this tragedy had shattered her faith in God. She could find no rhyme or reason in the senseless loss of her beloved brother, and although she had believed in God all her life, when her brother was killed she lost that belief—suddenly sure that no God could exist given such a tragedy. Religion, she decided, was "bullshit."

Life is fraught with joys and perils, and sometimes random people get drunk and drive home without hitting anyone or anything,
but sometimes they plow into a young man and kill him. It just
might be your younger brother. This student said to me that she
was sure that there is no God, there was only life—a mix of luck
and good fortune on the one hand; sadness, poor choices, and
devastating accidents on the other.

Such tragedies seem to produce an intriguing bifurcation. For
most humans, the death of a loved one does little to erode their
faith in God or love of their religion, and it can even make it
stronger. But for others, it leads them on the straight and sparsely
populated road to apostasy.

Beatrice grew up in Quebec but now lives in Seattle. She is 39,
married, has three kids, and works as a sales account manager.
She was raised Catholic, and she regularly attended church year
after year. She believed in God, prayed regularly, and was confirmed as a teenager. Although she was married in the Catholic
Church, this was done solely to please her father—for by the time
of her marriage, she was already estranged from her religion.
Today, she identifies as an atheist. The first chink in her religious
armor was the death of her mother:

> When I was about 13 or 14, my mom was diagnosed with breast cancer. . . . She
> had a mastectomy and they sort of thought that she was in remission. Then a
> couple of years later they found out that she actually wasn't in remission—it
> had spread further and her prognosis was not good. Then, you know, within a
> year of that she passed away. So, I was 16 and my brother and sister, like, 14
> and 13. I remember being very confused and very angry with God and not
> understanding how this could happen and how could . . . you know, I talked to
> him like, "What did I do wrong?" Why would God take her away from us . . . you
> know, all of that kind of stuff. You could think "God, God, God" and that all of
> this is part of his plan, but then you sort of like—why this painful kind of
> thing? I would say that's when my faith started to kind of . . . I started to
> question my faith. . . . You know, like that was the first time when I was really
> angry. But I guess I wasn't questioning his existence at that point, I was just
> sort of questioning, you know, why would he make this happen to me when I'd

been so good?... The day that she passed away, of course, our priest... he came to talk to us and I remember specifically not buying in to what he was saying of, like, trying to answer our questions of why she died. He said something like, "Well, she was in pain and now she's no longer in pain and she's in a better place" and this and that. I sort of just remember going, "Ahh, I don't quite buy this...."

Haneefa, age 26, is from Afghanistan, although she has lived in numerous countries—Austria, Kenya, Guam, and others—because her father worked for an international company for many years. Today she lives in Southern California, and is working toward a PhD in history. Haneefa was a Muslim for most of her life, but she no longer identifies as such. "I'm definitely an atheist," she explained, and she does not even consider herself Muslim in a cultural or ethnic sense. There were many sources of her apostasy, such as her five-year relationship with a nonbelieving, nonreligious boyfriend, the fact that her father was never all that devout or committed, and her experiences living in so many countries outside of Afghanistan, where she made friends with kids and families from all walks of life and all kinds of backgrounds. But the crucial, decisive moment when she knew she no longer believed was in the immediate wake of her mother's unexpected death:

My mom actually passed away very suddenly from pneumonia when I was 20.... Right after she passed away I did a lot of prayers because everybody has that—you know, the 40-day mourning. So I thought I should pray. I should pray because everybody's telling me to pray.... I did it for maybe a week, and then I kind of just prayed at night—just hoping that she's safe in heaven. Then all of a sudden—I don't know why—but I was just, like, I don't feel anything. I don't feel that she went anywhere. I thought that my prayers were useless—I'm just wasting my time. And I remember that all my questions about heaven and afterlife and everything when I was younger just were unanswered. At that moment—maybe over the span of three months—I all of a sudden let go of religion.... Because I just didn't feel anything, you know. I didn't believe that she went anywhere else. I think the belief in an afterlife is

central to religion, and that part—I just didn't feel it and I didn't believe in it.
So I let go of religion.

Josh was raised in a conservative Jewish household. His parents kept kosher, following the rabbinic dietary restrictions of observant Jews. They observed the Jewish holidays—especially the weekly Sabbath—and Josh attended a private Jewish school in which prayers to God and a study of the Jewish sacred texts were enmeshed with the otherwise secular curriculum. Today, although he maintains a sort of open spirituality, Josh no longer believes in the particulars of Judaism. He no longer believes that there is a God, he certainly does not believe in the power of prayer, and although he recognizes that he is Jewish in terms of his heritage and background, he doesn't consider himself religious anymore. And the main source of his apostasy was the inefficacy of prayer in the face of his mother's untimely death:

> *She died when I was nine. And I would say that's probably a big part of my*
> *divergence from Judaism.... She had brain cancer ... you know, as a little kid*
> *my dad would tell me all the time, you know, "Pray for her—like—pray and*
> *she'll be OK." And, you know I would try to...I would say the prayers,*
> *thinking about her, and I would occasionally just look at God and be like,*
> *"God, like, give us something to work with here, like, do something." And... he*
> *didn't do anything. So it was just kind of like: what does praying mean? Like,*
> *what does God mean? I think that was probably the biggest catalyst that*
> *really just, like, showed me at an early age that like I was kinda just taking*
> *this whole idea of God for granted and that, like—it's like—is he really out*
> *there? Is there really someone there?*

Personal tragedy has been a problem for religious believers ever since the first flames from the first holy bonfire accidentally caught the first shaman's hut on fire, burning his children within. When such things happen, the best a religious believer can cling to is the thought that "it's all in God's hands" or it's all "God's will." Such sentiments are embedded within the notion that, even in the face of inexplicable tragedy, there remains a deeper divine meaning or purpose, however hard to fathom. But for a minority of believers, such sentiments just don't work in the face of the acute pain of personal loss.

When one's marriage falls apart, or when prayer fails to work, or when one experiences the tragic death of a loved one—all of these can lead to a loss of belief. Faithful, religious adherents who find themselves confronted with painful or debilitating situations in life that seem at odds with—or contrary to—what they would expect can lose their belief in God. Such apostasy is often predicated upon a feeling of being forsaken, and seriously so. When one's life is wracked with troubles, it is possible to surmise: "If I am doing everything right in God's eyes and have committed my heart to him, then my personal life should be working out better, as one is taught to expect. And since it isn't, then maybe there isn't a God after all." If one's earnest prayers aren't answered, it might lead one to think: "If there is a God who answers prayers, as one is taught, then he would answer my prayer, and since he doesn't, I don't believe in him anymore." And finally, when one experiences the premature death of a loved one, he or she is apt to conclude: "If there is a loving, all-powerful God, as one is taught, then he wouldn't let young, good people die prematurely from random diseases, and since this occurs, I don't believe anymore."

*   *   *

Stories like these are ripe for analysis.

First, there is the very real possibility that—had certain things not happened in these people's lives—they may not have lost their faith. Sure, religion eventually stopped making sense for these people, but only in response to, or in the wake of, certain events. Today, David can wax on about how illogical this or that biblical story is. And yet these biblical stories didn't strike him as illogical or problematic for many, many years. Today he can debunk the story of Noah's ark as being so implausible as to be nothing more than a fairy tale, and yet he believed in this "fairy tale" for more than half his life. Something happened to change his perspective. Something happened to tighten the screws and change the wiring of his internal credulity meter. What happened was this: his life didn't work out so well. His wife cheated on him, then divorced him, and he found himself stuck in a series of dead-end jobs, with little money to pay for even basic utilities. Thus, it wasn't really the manifest absurdity of the story of Noah's ark that caused him to view Christian beliefs with a skeptical eye. Rather, it was misfortune. This leads us to wonder what David's religious identity might be today if things had actually worked out differently for him. What if the wife he had initially found had been committed, sweet, and faithful? What if their life together had been loving and warm? What if his career had been more lucrative and satisfying? Maybe he would have seen all of this as evidence of Jehovah's blessings. Perhaps he would have seen his success as a testament to the true religious vision of the Jehovah's Witnesses. And what about Barry? Maybe if his marriage had been a success, he might never have questioned his belief in and obedience to God, or his dutiful Catholicism. What if Beatrice's mother hadn't died of cancer? What if Penny's cat had actually come home, safe and sound? For each story shared by the men and women in this chapter, we are left wondering if they would have still rejected their faith if certain key elements in their lives had been different. Perhaps they would have, but perhaps not.

A second noteworthy aspect of these stories is the underlying theme of God not being wholly decent, not being wholly upstanding, not being an ethically responsive deity. There is, indeed, an underlying element of betrayal in these stories, of people feeling let down by the Lord—forsaken. For David and Barry, their difficulties led them to see God as not holding up his end of things. They had been humble servants, believing and worshipping as children of God, and yet God didn't look after them as a loving, powerful parent ought to. He didn't make sure that things in their lives were okay. It seemed to be quite the opposite. For Penny and Carol, their prayers went unheeded. God didn't respond. Why not? Weren't they his good, dutiful followers? Wasn't he a God who answered earnest prayers? Apparently not. For Beatrice, Haneefa, and Josh, the death of their mothers caused a serious crisis in their understanding of God; he was either too callous or too impotent to save their mothers. Either way, this was not the sort of God they had initially been raised to believe in.

For all of these men and women, at some point God came to be seen as unfair, unjust. His failure to make sure that things worked out, to answer earnest prayers, to keep young mothers alive— these all suggest a God that is either unloving, ineffective, or both. Such sentiments were deeply disappointing to these individuals. They led to a sense of betrayal or even heartbreak.

However, despite the fact that many individuals whom I interviewed cited instances of personal misfortune as a catalyst for their eventual rejection of religion, it is essential to recognize that widespread misfortune definitely does not cause secularization at the macro, societal level. In fact, it is exactly within those countries rife with misfortune, disease, poverty, and death that religion is the strongest. The most convincing research along these lines—concerning why some societies are highly religious and others are relatively secular—comes from the political scientists Pippa Norris and Ronald Inglehart. In their book *Sacred and Secular*, they have convincingly shown that widespread vulnerability to misfortune is key. When the bulk of people in a given society experience high levels of insecurity, hunger, homelessness, disease, disorder, unemployment, crime, vulnerability to natural disasters, and so on—such societies tend to be very religious. Conversely, when the bulk of people in a given society experience relatively secure and stable lives wherein their material and communal needs are well met and life is characterized by peace, prosperity, and general well-being—such societies tend to be among the most secular on earth.

Thus, we are faced with somewhat of a potential paradox. On the micro, individual level, personal misfortune can serve as a direct cause of apostasy. Yet on the macro, societal level, an abundance of misfortune seems to strengthen religiosity, not weaken it. There are two ways to reconcile this paradox. The first is to understand that the reasons for apostasy articulated by individuals in the recounting of their own personal narratives are going to be quite different from statistical averages, demographic trends, or sociological rates of well-being/misfortune and secularity/religiosity in large national populations. It may very well be the case that when misfortune and insecurity are widespread, pervasive, and deeply entrenched in a given society, the overall result is increased religiosity, while perhaps for individuals living in relatively secure and stable societies, personal misfortune can suddenly become a catalyst for apostasy. But another, perhaps less complicated way to reconcile the apparent paradox is to simply remember that most people who experience personal misfortune do not go on to reject religion. After all, if personal misfortune—in and of itself—caused apostasy, religion would have died out long ago. The reality is that most deeply religious men and women who are committed to the Lord, at some point, face tough life circumstances—such as a failed marriage or financial difficulties. Most experience the failure of prayer. Many experience the untimely death of a loved one. And for most religious men and women, these unfortunate phenomena do not shatter their faith. They don't even shake it. But for some rare men and women, they do both.

4

⌁

To Be Mormon, or Not to Be

Cecilia and Andrew were both strong, devout Mormons for most of their lives. But not anymore.

I'd never met Cecilia before our interview. My father happened to be talking to an old friend of his about my research, and this friend mentioned that a neighbor of his used to be a Mormon. He said he thought that her rejection of Mormonism might have had something to do with the Mormon Church's active support of Proposition 8—the ballot initiative of 2008 that sought to make gay marriage illegal in the state of California. With my Dad's friend's help, I contacted Cecilia, and she agreed to do the interview, so long as confidentiality was absolutely guaranteed. She was quite worried that family members, friends, and other Mormons in her community might be able to identify her if they read this book—something she really, really didn't want to happen. I promised her that I would do my best to conceal her identity. I drove out to San Bernardino—a city of 200,000—and did the interview one weekday morning while her three sons were at school and her husband was at work.

Cecilia is 39 years old and looks positively Scandinavian. Things started a bit awkwardly when she asked me if she could get me anything and I said a cup of hot tea would be nice—forgetting that hot tea is not something Mormons typically drink, in accordance with one of the Mormon holy books, *Doctrines and Covenants*. Even though Cecilia has left the church, Mormon culture retains a hold on her. Hence, she didn't have any tea to offer me that morning. A glass of water sufficed.

Cecilia began by laying out her impressive Mormon credentials:

> Both my parents were raised in the church. I'm actually all the way back to Joseph Smith and Nauvoo time. So I'm probably sixth-generation LDS [Latter-Day Saints].... My grandfather was a bishop when I was a little girl. My grandmother has been primary president, in charge of all the children in the ward....So I grew up really active in the church, going to church every Sunday....I was a good girl and did everything I was ever supposed to do and never got in trouble in school and made good grades.

For the vast majority of her life, Cecilia was immersed in the Mormon religion and thoroughly committed to its ways. In addition to regularly attending church and Sunday school, throughout her teenage years she attended "seminary" classes, which provide theologically based instruction to LDS teenagers every morning before school. She was very active in whatever youth conferences, clubs, and activities were available at whatever age she happened to be. And she always studied the Book of Mormon, diligently. When she got to college, she dutifully enrolled in weekly "institute classes," for college-aged Mormons. While she was growing up, both her mother and father took on leadership roles within their local congregation—although Cecilia confessed that there was a brief time when her mother withdrew from the church for a few years when she was younger, for reasons she didn't care to go into. But aside from that brief blip, Cecilia and her family were enmeshed in the Mormon community to a degree that non-Mormons might find surprising. As Cecilia describes it, the Mormon community exists as a nearly separate world within the United States. It is a durable bubble of a subculture, where every week is laced with religious activities, special events, classes, outings, meetings, prayer, and worship. To walk away from this world is no easy task. Few Mormons ever do. But Cecilia is one of those few. She hasn't been to church now for about two years—which is quite something, given that she had gone to church several times a week, every week of her life, before then.

> *I would say for the first time in my whole life, I'm an outsider looking in. I've never . . . even when I've had moments of "ugh"—I've always been an insider. Mormonism is one of those things—you'll never not be LDS. It's shaped every memory of your childhood. It's so pervasive in your everyday life that you're never not going to be LDS. It's like a race almost; this is my ancestry. So for that reason I will always have that in me, that culture . . . that's always going to be there. If people ask me now, I say that I was "raised LDS." . . . But I don't know what else to say. . . . I just don't want to have somebody assume things about me, especially with the whole last election. I don't want that assumption on my head. So I'm trying to separate.*

I wondered about Cecilia's opinion of Joseph Smith, the founding visionary of the Mormon religion. I was curious: didn't she believe that he was a prophet of God who had been visited by the Lord, as well as Jesus and various angels, and who had—with the help of "seer-stones"—translated ancient golden plates upon which were to be found the holy scriptures that compose the Book of Mormon? As it turned out, these miraculous events at the heart of the Mormon faith were not that significant to Cecilia. Sure, she had claimed to believe them for nearly all her life, and when she went in for official interviews with high-ranking members of the church now and then—they would quiz her on whether she believed various claims of the church—she always said yes. But did she really, really believe it?

> *Whether I consciously thought that he [Joseph Smith] translated the plates, I don't know. However, throughout my life as I've gone in for interviews and they've asked me those questions—I have answered yes. But I never had any sort of witnessing affirmation that that had taken place. It was just like,*

"I can believe it." I never felt like I was lying either. I've actually heard people say, "Fake it until you make it." Now I think, oh my God, why didn't that send up flares in my brain? You mean, indoctrinate yourself? Brainwash yourself, basically? But it was put in a way that if you exercise faith first, then the witness will come next. That's all I was doing.

The more I spoke with Cecilia, the more clearly I understood that, for her, the specific details, the central creeds, the holy tenets of the Mormon religion—including Joseph Smith's supposed visions and miraculous deeds—were not pressing matters of concern, contemplation, or debate. Did she believe that God lives on a planet called Kolob, as Joseph Smith revealed? Did she believe that there are three levels of heaven (or "degrees of glory"): the celestial, terrestrial, and telestial? Did she believe that Jesus once visited North America and that the Garden of Eden was actually in western Missouri? Perhaps. Perhaps not. The many tenets of the Mormon religion just weren't all that important to her— never had been, really. They were just part of her broader religious life, culture, and heritage. And when I specifically asked her about such teachings and beliefs, I didn't get any harsh or pointed criticisms of doctrines she now considered false. In fact, she tended to casually change the subject—not because the questions made her uncomfortable, but rather, because they seemed unimportant. Thus, unlike many apostates, the matter of believing in various religious concepts, tenets, or miracles was never all that significant to Cecilia—not when she was inside Mormonism, nor now that she is on the outside. What caused her to leave her people, her community, and her church was not that the specific beliefs had somehow stopped making sense. It was a host of other issues.

The first was the underwear—or, to use the correct Mormon term, the "temple garments." All adult Mormons are expected to wear temple garments at all times. This special Mormon underwear consists of two pieces, the top one similar to a basic T-shirt that covers the stomach, back, torso, shoulders, and upper arms, and the bottom piece like a pair of long boxer shorts, extending down to just above the knees. They are worn as a symbolic reminder of the holy covenants made in Mormon temple ceremonies, as well as a reminder of an individual's relationship with Jesus Christ. And they are also viewed as a spiritual as well as literal source of protection; they are believed to be endowed with certain magical or spiritual powers that can protect the wearer from physical harm. No good Mormon takes off his or her undergarments for any reason, day or night, unless it is absolutely necessary. One day, Cecilia just couldn't stand it anymore.

> *I took them off. . . . That probably was the catalyst for everything, when I think about it. My grandma died three years ago. She suffered for several years and we helped take care of her, which was a horrible experience. It put me into a really bad depression. . . . I'd lay in bed and watch movies all day long. So I went to a therapist. She asked: what are your frustrations? I started to get where I didn't leave the house because I was so hot . . . you know, San Bernardino's hot. I'm a hot person anyway, and I sweat a lot. And I thought I'm already over-hot, I'm constantly wet—and so I would not leave the house because I'd think if I leave the house, in ten minutes I'm going to have sweat stains down to my waist. Then I'm totally psychologically uncomfortable in front of people because they wonder if I'm having a heart attack or something and that's why I'm sweating so profusely. . . . Anyway, I told the therapist that the undergarments were driving me crazy and she said, "Why don't you take them off?" I said because you're told your whole life that if you take them off you remove the protection that they give to you. Now, on a really normal, practical level, I knew they weren't made out of Kevlar. If somebody shoots you, you're going to die. Yet the myth in the church is that they have some sort of physical protection for you. . . . But then the less you wear them, the less you realize you don't feel any different. They weren't a reminder to me of my covenants. They were a reminder to me of how freaking hot and miserable I was! So I took them off with the idea that it was purely a physical thing. It was only because my body couldn't deal. I'd go to Wal-Mart and have hot flashes and feel like I was dying. So I went in and told my bishop that I was taking them off, and he was, of course, terrified at the thought. . . . So I took them off about three or four years ago. I've since gone to tank tops, so blatantly making it*

clear to everybody who knows I've been through the temple that I don't wear them. They see that as a declaration of apostasy.

Cecilia was also turned off by the church's politics: a conformity-laced conservatism permeated the Church of Jesus Christ of Latter-Day Saints and it made her feel alienated, uncomfortable, and even unwelcome.

> *We were kind of patted on the head as "silly little Democrats." Then comments would be made after George Bush won and they would say, "Oh, are you so sad?" So, things like that would bug me and I'd just come home from church thinking—ugh! Because now there's this weird thing of, you know, the "Lord's party is the Republicans" and it was so pervading. You know, the church really pats itself on the back for it. . . .*

A third factor in Cecilia's rejection of Mormonism—and the one that she stressed as being the most significant—was Proposition 8. If any specific issue ultimately pushed her away from her religion, this was undoubtedly it. In 2004, the mayor of San Francisco, Gavin Newsom, began allowing same-sex couples to marry in defiance of California law. Then, in 2008, the California Supreme Court struck down that law as unconstitutional, granting gays and lesbians the legal right to marry. Thousands did. Proposition 8 attempted to revoke that right without running afoul of the courts. It declared: "Only marriage between a man and a woman is valid or recognized in California." Proposition 8 passed in the fall of 2008, by a margin of 52.24% to 47.76%—thanks in part to religious conservative religious groups, who were its biggest supporters. The Mormon Church was the most prominent among them. The church galvanized hundreds of thousands of people, and raised millions of dollars, to make gay marriage illegal in California.

For some Mormons like Cecilia, it wasn't just that the Mormon Church took a stand against gay marriage that was a problem—it was that there seemed to be an obsession with the issue, a mean-spirited fixation on defeating gay marriage that went beyond mere advocacy or moral instruction. Week after week, month after month, sermons and speeches were devoted to the topic. Donations were sought incessantly. Political activism against gay marriage was encouraged. And lawn signs were distributed with vigor—often at the exit of the church parking lot, so that everyone leaving church on Sundays would be handed a sign on their way out. Those who didn't want to take and put an anti–gay marriage sign on their lawns were seen as morally suspect.

> Prop 8 was like just over the head with it—every meeting. You know, it's a three-hour time block that you go to. Every single hour was devoted to it and was—if not the topic of the whole thing—then at least opening remarks thanking you for going out knocking door to door . . . you know, "We really need to do the Lord's work here" . . . over and over. . . . And so stuff like that, I couldn't deal with it anymore. I didn't want my kids to hear that anymore.

Cecilia's husband felt the same way. He simply could not understand why the church was so obsessed with stopping gay marriage. Like Cecilia, he felt that homosexuals should be able to marry whoever they wanted, because it was their right as adult citizens. If the church did not want to honor such marriages, fine. But why make such a big deal out of it? But Cecilia and her husband found precious few others within their community who shared these sentiments. It is worth mentioning here that many people, about one third of those I interviewed, cited the controversy over gay rights—their religion's condemnation of homosexuality, their church's activism against gays and lesbians, or their coreligionists lack of support for gay rights—as a key ingredient in their apostasy.[1]

There was one other factor that helps explain Cecilia's alienation: sex.

Towards the end of the interview, I asked her some questions about her experiences with sex in relation to her religion, and lots of thoughts and memories came pouring out. They were mostly negative. In fact, Cecilia spoke of the church's approach to sex as personally damaging. There were specific teachings of the Mormon Church that were hammered into her for years, and the one that was most prominent was that women should remain virgins until marriage. The best thing a Mormon girl can do is to keep herself "pure" for her "glorious" temple wedding. And she should always remember that "carnal lust" is immoral, unhealthy, unsaintly, and should be avoided at all times. Sexual urges were simply to be stifled. All of these teachings, drummed into her for years, had the effect of limiting not only Cecilia's sexual experiences prior to marriage, but also her emotions and feelings about sex in general. It would have a decidedly negative impact on her married life.

You get the lessons on—if you have sex before marriage, then you're like a board that's had a nail put in it. You can remove the nail through repentance, but the hole's still going to be there. . . . So it was always "keep yourself pure, keep yourself holy." I was always kind of a sensual person and made out with a ton of guys, but I drew the line. And there were times when I thought: "If I wasn't Mormon, man, I would be a whore." But in reality, now looking back as an adult, I wouldn't have been a whore. I probably would have had sex with more than one person . . . like maybe two! To me, that was a whore, you'd be a whore! . . . You know, you just put a cap on that. So I grew up thinking that if I keep myself pure, I will in turn deserve somebody who is pure and then everything will be perfect. Anyway . . . I met Jeremy when I was 18. . . . With Jeremy, we went farther—had we been totally honest in our temple interview, we would not have been able to get married in the temple. . . . Yet I wasn't willing to tell the truth because the ramifications of it would have been more than I could take at 20. . . . I was terrified of eternal retribution for lying to get into the temple. . . . For the next five years I cried myself to sleep every night over this huge sin that I compounded by—"we've already screwed it up, we can never go back." . . . It was five years of—honestly—I thought I was just going to go insane over this guilt. Crying and crying and praying and praying . . . just "please, please, please." That was all I could articulate, just "please, please, please take this away. Take this guilt away, make it okay."

* * *

Andrew didn't have a problem with underwear. But as for the other issues that troubled Cecilia—he could definitely relate. And as a gay man, these issues were deeply personal. Andrew is 35 years old and lives in a small town outside of Los Angeles, where he works as a physical therapist and nutritionist. He grew up in Phoenix, Arizona, and he was one of ten kids. He describes his family as one of the most upstanding and respected within the Mormon community in Phoenix.

> We were model Mormons. We went to church every Sunday. We paid our 10% tithe on our gross, not our net. We had "family home evening" every Monday night, which is the night that Mormon families set aside to just spend time together. We had daily scripture study, like every morning. My mother was a stay-at-home mom, you know, with ten kids and my father was the sole provider.... I remember having a family counsel because we were going to go on a walk, you know, just for a few blocks on a Sunday afternoon, and I wanted to know if I could wear roller skates. We had to call a family counsel because I might have too much fun, and we weren't supposed to necessarily play on the Sabbath.

Like Cecilia's, Andrew's world was permeated by Mormon religion and culture, from church services to youth groups, from family rituals to the expectations of tithing, from scriptural study to missionary work. And he embraced it all. He relished it all. He loved his religion.

> I was a hyper-Mormon. I was totally just so knee-deep in it. In fact, I really think—I really do believe this, I sincerely believe this—that of all the siblings that I have, of all the kids—I think I was the most spiritually and religiously sensitive. You know, I think even my mother used to tell me that. I mean, I would—I have very vivid memories of weeping. Praying and weeping because I felt so bad for Satan. I felt compassion for Satan because he couldn't be forgiven. I mean, I remember that as a kid.

Today, Andrew is no longer a member of the Church of Jesus Christ of Latter-Day Saints.

My membership was rescinded. The technical term for that—and this is harsh—is "stricken from the records of the church." I don't know if my family knows. I think some of them do. I got a letter one day—certified mail—from the bishop or the stake president at the local church. And it said they were summoning me to a disciplinary court. This is where a person who has broken some Mormon laws stands in front of a group of 12 men and they decide what your fate is in the church. I mean, it's not friendly. Because—and this was the quote—because I was "living a lifestyle that was contrary to the law and order of the church." Living with another guy. I wrote them back....I took some time to really thoughtfully write them back and to tell them that this was really their drama. It wasn't mine. And they needed to do what they needed to do and I would obviously not be there. And I sent it off. Shortly thereafter, I got a letter that said, very well, we've received your letter and want you to know that your membership has been stricken from the records of the church, that your baptism has been... That was the moment of just—the ground dropping out. It was interesting because it dropped—it's so peculiar to describe this because it didn't mean anything to me, but it meant every- thing. It was like my history—it was like my whole history was gone. All of my friends growing up were Mormon and that was gone. I mean suddenly— just suddenly. Just—the reality of it was really heavy. It was like they had stolen my identity right out from underneath me. It was this feeling of groundlessness, like I had nothing to stand on. I had no idea who I was or what I believed in. I wasn't prepared for that. I wasn't prepared for it to have an effect on me like it did.

The cause of Andrew's trouble with Mormonism—or as may be more accurate, Mormonism's trouble with Andrew—was his homo- sexuality. This issue was the ineradicable, rusty blade that excised him from his beloved faith.

I had my first crush on a man—on another guy—when I was in fifth grade. I didn't know that's what it was at the time, but it was...I mean, for me, it wasn't like I woke up one day and said, "Oh my gosh, I'm gay." I mean, I didn't do that. I had lots of girlfriends. Lots. In fact, I was practically engaged twice and I broke it off both times.... I knew there was something that wasn't right. In my teen years... I knew I was attracted to guys, I knew I did.... You know, when I masturbated, it was fantasizing about men. It was never girls—never.

And your dreams, erotic dreams were ... ?

Almost always men—almost always. You know, it doesn't take a degree to figure out that "Oh my gosh, I'm more attracted to men than to women. . . . Anyway, so through high school I had girlfriends and I was fantasizing about my teachers—male teachers and just thinking, "Gosh this doesn't add up. This doesn't add up." Try as I might—fasting and prayer would not— it would not leave. It would not leave. I mean, I was about as devout as it got. I mean, I was terrified of how bad masturbation was killing my ability to receive the spirit. That's what you're taught, is that if you masturbate, the spirit of the Lord can't really be with you.

Wow, that's heavy.

It's totally heavy, because I was a fierce masturbator. It was my favorite extracurricular activity. It was my sport [laughter].

Andrew tried various Mormon-recommended remedies to keep himself from masturbating, such as tying his right arm to the frame of his bed. But it didn't work.

Because it was like, okay, I'm trying desperately to lose this attraction to men, but I can't stop jerking off. I just can't. Because I just love it. I do it in my sleep if I don't do it when I'm awake, you know. And I can't stop thinking about guys. And it's complicated by the fact that every time I do that it cuts me off from the Lord. It's terrible. So it's like—I'm hopeless. Part of being Mormon is sitting down with your bishop, who's like the pastor of the congregation, and answering very candid questions that he asks you: "So do you masturbate?" Yeah. I mean, it's embarrassing . . . and we're having these really open discussions. What he told me was, "If you starve it, it'll die. If you starve it, it will die." . . . Yeah, it was terrible. It really, really, really was . . . I mean, I'm trying so hard and God knows how hard I'm trying. In the Mormon Church— fuck them for this!! There is this terrible, horrible, horrible teaching from one of the prophets: "How can you say it cannot be done unless your knuckles are bloody and your head is bruised from trying?" Basically, you can never, ever, ever, ever give up. Never. And I hate that—it's another thing I hate. It's like, I was—I mean, spiritually—I was battered and bruised terribly. I mean, I was so wounded, so sensitive. I was a very sensitive kid, obviously, you know. It just made it worse because it was like I'm not trying hard enough. What more could I do? I passed out in school because I was fasting for days on end that this would go away, that I would somehow be normal, that I would be healed from this homoerotic stuff. And I passed out in class and had to be wheelchaired out by my mother.

After high school, although still struggling with his desire to masturbate and his attraction to men, Andrew went on a two-year mission to win converts.

I had struck a deal with God that I would give him two years of my life and I would be the best damn missionary that there could be and He would make me straight. That was the agreement. That's exactly what I wanted. That's exactly what I wanted.

Andrew was sent off to Moldova, a small country in Eastern Europe.

I mastered the Moldovan language. . . . I was the pride and joy of that missionary center. I baptized more people than I can remember. I worked my ass off. I worked so hard. You know, most missionaries they would get onto the metro, they would get on the trains and they would sit down and just relax until they got to the next stop. Not me. Book of Mormon in hand, I would go to the first person I saw: "Hey, can I talk to you for a minute? Have you ever heard of the Book of Mormon?" Every single time. I mean, I was Rambo in missionary clothes, you know. I gained a reputation for it. I got commendation from the mission president when they sent me back . . . you know: "This is one of the best missionaries we have ever had." And I had crushes on guys while I was on my mission . . . so I had this, like, double personality where I was just a Mormon Nazi just trying so hard to do everything right and I was praying every day, and then, on the other hand, I'm in the bathroom jerking off and feeling terrible about it and repenting and fasting for another day. Yeah, it's like bingeing. It's like bulimia—it's like spiritual bulimia. So I got home from my mission—felt like a success and the ultimate failure at the same time. . . . Everyone was so proud of me . . . my parents were so proud of me. How do you turn to someone and say, "You know what? It's fake, it's not real, it's tarnished. . . ." How do you say that? You don't. You just repent and you keep fasting and praying. I started dating other girls and, you know, I would take them out to dinner and—I would find the waiter hot! I was very angry and very depressed but unable to share it with anybody . . . period . . . very, very alone. . . . Not long after then, the anti-gay initiative came out, you know. The anti-gay initiative banning gay marriage, and it was really being pushed in church. . . . It really, really bothered me. And one day in particular, I think it broke me because I left church and I went to my friend's house and I just cried—I think for an hour straight. I laid out paper towels; I had a knife and was going to slit my wrists. I was sorry, I didn't want to leave a mess, so I had made sure I was going to do it on the tile and not the carpet. Oh my God, I'd never been so close before. But I felt worthless and useless and terrible and unsavable and I was just that close. Then it just hit me. And the reason I didn't was because I had this revelation that even if I did—even if I had committed suicide and I was dead and gone . . . I would still be an embarrassment to my parents, to my family. That "the reason he was gone was because he was gay." You know, that was—it was like, wow, not even death can take that away. Not even death. This ultimate disgrace can't even be erased by death. I just dropped the knife and I cried for another 30 minutes and grabbed all the paper towels and I threw them away. . . . I no longer had a choice. It was either die a Mormon or leave the church, and so I left. I just stopped going.

If you hadn't been gay or you hadn't had homoerotic feelings, do you think you'd still be a Mormon?

Absolutely. If it hadn't been for this—meaning my being gay—I would be very happily married, a very happy Mormon with a white picket fence and 4.5 children and a dog. I really would. I liked being Mormon, I liked everything about it. Except I couldn't be me. . . . Now I think that the Church of Jesus Christ of Latter-Day Saints does more harm in the world than good.

Do you still believe in any church teachings? Do you still believe that Joseph Smith was visited by divine beings and that he really translated golden plates that subsequently floated into heaven—or do you now think it was all a made-up hoax?

> *That's hard for me. That's probably an unexpected response, but...I really don't know.... The rational part of me says, "No, obviously it's not." Another part of me says, "Well, it could very well be—there may be spiritual realms and there may be spiritual beings in those spiritual realms."... So is it possible that Joseph Smith saw something? Yeah, I think it is. I really think it is. Is it possible that what Joseph Smith created when he started putting this church together is largely from his imagination—very active imagination? Yeah, I think it is. Is it possible that the gold plates existed? Whoosh, I don't know ... maybe ... probably not ... maybe. I don't know how to answer it. But I'm so comfortable with not knowing, and that's something I've learned from Buddhism.*

*   *   *

In some ways, Andrew and Cecilia had similar journeys from active, faithful Mormonism to apostasy.

First and foremost, unlike many other apostates, neither of them had any interest in actively critiquing the religious beliefs of Mormons. Neither of them wanted to condemn Joseph Smith as a conman or even to dismiss him as a misguided individual with an active imagination. Neither of them felt the urge to mock Mormon teachings or to debunk the Book of Mormon. These were simply not matters of pressing concern.

This is important, for it is specific beliefs that often baffle outsiders, but they can be more or less nonissues for insiders. Indeed, insider and outsider perspectives often talk right past one another on this exact issue. For outsiders—that is, non-Mormons or just plain secular folk—it is the specifically outlandish doctrines, teachings, and beliefs of Mormonism that are worthy of scrutiny and discussion. Thus, for most non-Mormons and secular skeptics, the major, underlying question concerning Mormonism thus tends to be: how can they believe this stuff? However, it seems that, for at least some insiders, these beliefs are not necessarily things to be fervently held, passionately accepted, or heavily defended. Rather, they are just part of a much broader religious enterprise, grounded principally upon family, community, history, heritage, ritual, and a host of other ingredients that all serve to create a powerful worldview—and world—that most Mormons find to be sustaining, comforting, and admirable. Sure, the beliefs are significant—at least on the surface. All Mormons are expected to believe in this or that creed—and they are periodically quizzed on these beliefs, with the articulation of affirmative answers as par for the course. But I got the distinct impression from Andrew and Cecilia—and from others whom I have interviewed—that some Mormons just sort of casually accept, mildly subscribe to, or generally just sort of go along with these beliefs uncritically, apathetically, and almost even symbolically, because they value the rest of what their religion offers. For Andrew and Cecilia, the specific religious beliefs that outsiders and skeptics find so hard to digest were marginal or relatively insignificant. To be Mormon was about so much more—above and beyond these beliefs—as was the life-changing decision to stop being Mormon.

The second similarity I'd like to highlight is that both Andrew and Cecilia, as a result of their apostasy, have become "deviants." By dubbing Cecilia and Andrew deviant, I am not putting forth a negative moral judgment. I mean no disrespect. For sociologists, the term "deviant" is simply a value-neutral term used to designate someone who does not conform to his or her group's norms or values. A deviant is someone who doesn't do what everyone else is doing and who refuses to believe, say, or go along with what everyone else does. Sometimes deviance is undoubtedly bad, bizarre, or evil, but other times it can be markedly moral, humane, or courageous.[2]

The deviance of Cecilia and Andrew was predicated upon nothing particularly spectacular, flagrant, or dangerous. They just stopped going to church. They stopped identifying as Mormon. And this decision was largely based on their valuing individuality over group conformity. They both felt compelled to pursue their own paths, to be true to themselves, to adhere to their own consciences—despite the consequences. And there are always consequences to deviance. To paraphrase Erving Goffman, to be a deviant is to often find that one's social identity is "spoiled." Given that conformity is the Velcro of communal life, those individuals who don't conform to their community's norms, mores, or values will always experience some sort of negative reaction or social sanction. It may be subtle or overt, ranging from mild disapproval or bemused gossip to debilitating stigmatization, shunning exclusion, absolute expulsion, or worse. As an apostate—and thus deviant within the Mormon culture—Andrew was officially excommunicated ("stricken from the records of the church"), and he subsequently lost many friends and family members who wanted nothing more to do with him. There were similar consequences for Cecilia. Although she has not (yet) been excommunicated, she has lost many friends in the wake of her apostasy—and her relationships with many of her relatives have been strained. Some cousins have cut her off completely, treating her as though she no longer exists; one has charged her with being evil incarnate. The last thing I remember from my interview with Cecilia—a vivid memory, to be sure—was the pained look on her face as she was saying goodbye to me on her front porch. It was a look of worry, as she pleaded with me to make sure to change key aspects of her identity so that others would not "know it was her," which she feared would only deepen her isolation and stigmatization.[3]

Of all those I interviewed, the ex-Mormons seemed to be the most concerned about being "found out" in the wake of this book's publication. They were the only ones who still cared deeply about what their friends, families, and coreligionists might think of their apostasy. Nearly everyone else whom I interviewed didn't seem to care at all—ex-Catholics, ex-Protestants, ex-Jehovah's Witnesses, ex-Jews—and they didn't really mind much if anyone knew of their apostasy, and they didn't worry about offending or upsetting any of their former coreligionists.

Not so for Cecilia or Andrew. They continued to feel the pain and isolation of their apostasy, and they feared being "outed" by my research. They worried that their words or stories might upset or offend other Mormons. And they didn't want to bring any additional shame to their families. Why, out of all the individuals from a variety of religious backgrounds, were the former Mormons most pained by and worried about their apostasies? I attribute it to the extent that Mormonism really is a near "total world"—an all-encompassing subculture of religion and heritage that is held together by, among other things, a highly regulated and perpetually enforced cultural-religious-political conformity. To be an active Mormon is to be part of a deep and extensive web of social and familial connections, perpetually reinforced by obedience to leaders and allegiance to the group. As such, ex-Mormons feel a pointed sense of loss, emptiness, and social rejection when they step away. They become deviants within the Mormon community, and for this they often pay a heavy price. Another ex-Mormon I interviewed, Caleb, age 62, said several of his adult children will no longer communicate with him, and they have barred him from ever seeing his grandchildren. As he explained:

> There's a social price I pay. Friends that have known me for years have nothing to do with me—and to the children that I raised—I'm an evil to be avoided.

I suspect that there are many people out there, within Mormonism as well as every other religion, who would like to reject their religion and become apostates but don't—specifically because they couldn't handle the social stigma and the rejection of their friends and family.

Similarities aside, there are important differences in the stories of Cecilia and Andrew. The main difference is that for Cecilia, her rejection of Mormonism was based on a hodge-podge of several issues that accumulated over many years, until the Mormon Church's aggressive involvement with Proposition 8 became the straw that broke the camel's back. In short, her apostasy was

truly multicausal. This was the case for most people I interviewed—their apostasy was seldom about one thing. Rather, it
was the result of an accumulation of factors. But for Andrew,
there was indeed one single cause, and only one: his homosexuality. As he said, were it not for his being gay, he'd be a "very
happy Mormon with a white picket fence and 4.5 children and a
dog." But because homosexuals are not accepted as members of
the church, and because Mormons regard homosexuality as ultimately something quite sinful, Andrew had to choose between
his love of Mormonism and his love of other men. It wasn't an
easy choice. He almost killed himself over it. In the end, he
managed to pull through but he lost his faith in the process.

Andrew's story is not uncommon. Hundreds of thousands of
men and women the world over are born and raised into strongly
traditional, strictly conservative, or fundamentalist religious
groups and, realizing that they are gay or lesbian, face painful
and wrenching decisions as they get older. Many of them cannot
bear the burden, and they kill themselves. One recent federal
government report found that gay male adolescents within the
United States are two to three times more likely than heterosexual teens to attempt suicide. Many others try desperately to
suppress or deny their homosexuality, and they attempt to live
their lives as straight men or women, a choice that often leads to
depression, alcoholism, and entrenched despondency because
lives built upon lies are never happy or healthy. Many others, like
Andrew, choose to live honestly and freely. But in order to do so,
they must—often sadly and reluctantly—reject the religion that
is, in essence, rejecting them. It comes as no surprise that studies
find that apostasy is markedly higher among homosexuals, particularly gay men, than heterosexuals.[4]

Sex and sexuality, as I was to find out, were often integrally
tied to people's religious identities and with their irreligious identities as well.

5

Sex and Secularity

"My Dad even went out and got me a high-class hooker."[1] Frank is one of my cousin's wife's best friends. I see him about twice a year, whenever there is some family get-together at my cousin's house. He is in his early forties, he's very muscular and clean-cut, and he works as a probation officer. He was raised in a conservative Christian home. And he loved Jesus while growing up. But he also loved looking at JC Penney catalogues that would come in the mail on occasion, especially the ones that featured men in underwear. If a particularly good catalogue came, Frank would take it down into the basement and masturbate. This was when he was 14 years old. He knew it was sinful. But he just couldn't help it.

Throughout his teenage years, Frank struggled with the conflict that arose between his faith and his sexuality. He expressed one openly, and the other covertly. He attended church; he participated in religious youth groups, ceremonies, and rituals; and he believed wholeheartedly in the Bible. But he kept his attraction to men a secret, and it only festered. Even while Frank was a dutiful, pious student at the nearby Christian college he attended, his homosexuality churned within, and he often hooked up with other closeted gay students for friendship, romance, and intimacy.

"You had boyfriends at your Christian college?" I asked, mildly astonished.

"Oh, sure. We found each other. It wasn't hard."

What was hard was keeping his homosexuality a secret. Once he was in his early twenties, his love for men just couldn't be hidden any longer. Frank finally told his father, who was shocked and saddened. Frank's dad happened to be a very well-respected church deacon—a leader in their congregation—and he considered Frank's homosexuality to be a true calamity, both personally and spiritually. So in a desperate attempt to "cure" his son, Frank's father spent a lot of money on a high-end prostitute. He paid her to accompany Frank to Hawaii for a two-week, all-expenses-paid vacation. Her task: make Frank straight.

"What happened?"

> Oh, she was great. A really nice woman. Very kind. We didn't have sex together, but we partied a lot together—we went out to the bars at night and picked up men. It was a lot of fun.

Today, Frank is no longer a Christian. He is an out-of-the-closet gay man, living freely with his companion of more than 15 years. His family has come to accept him, although his young nieces and nephews are not allowed to sit on his lap at family get-togethers.

But homosexuals are not the only ones who struggle with issues concerning sex and religion.

Consider Geraldine—a heterosexual mother of three. One night, my wife and I were hosting a dinner party. Several couples were over, some that I knew well, others not so well. We were all sitting at a big table in our backyard, enjoying pasta, asparagus, and a cool breeze. At one point, I went back into the house to fetch a bottle of wine, and Geraldine was in the kitchen, pouring herself a glass of water. Geraldine was one of the guests whom I didn't know very well. Her kids went to school with my kids, but that was the sum total of our connection. As we headed back outside she asked,

"What do you teach, Phil?"

"Sociology and some classes on religion."

"Is that what you study—religion?"

"Yes—well, I used to. I'm actually studying secular people these days."

"What do you mean—like, atheists?"

"Yeah. Right now I'm studying apostates—people who were once religious but are no longer."

"Oh, well, you're looking at one. I used to be a born-again Christian."

"You were?"

"But I gave that up a long time ago."

"What happened?"

"I wanted to have sex."

It was then that we reached the dinner table. The next morning I called Geraldine and asked her if I could come over to her house and do an interview. She readily agreed.

Geraldine is 46 years old. She works as an accountant. She was raised in Orange County, California, by Nixon-supporting, lawn-tending parents. Her father was a real estate agent and her mother was an elementary school librarian. Geraldine was raised a Christian, that is, a Protestant—Catholics were considered non-Christians. As for her own religiosity growing up:

I very much believed in God and Jesus and I prayed all the time.

Did you think that Jesus was literally resurrected and that he saves us from our sins and all of that?

I think as a child I did, because that's what we were taught, you know. Why would they lie to you?

When she was in high school, Geraldine became born-again. She accepted Jesus Christ as her personal savior. She went to Bible study regularly and joined a nondenominational, Evangelical youth movement that stressed a deeply spiritual connection to God through Jesus, as well as the absolute inerrancy of the Bible. She also spent several Easter vacations in Mexico as a missionary, trying to convert the poor, misguided Catholics there into becoming "true" Christians. But Geraldine liked boys. She had many boyfriends during high school. But as a devout Christian, she always strictly limited the physical contact between her and her boyfriends, curtailing anything that might lead them to go too far. She knew that premarital sex was sinful, and she believed that anything beyond holding hands or mild kissing was too lustful to meet with God's approval. Her late teenage years were thus spent in various levels of emotional, physical, and/or spiritual agony: she had boyfriends she was attracted to, but she worked so hard to control her physical desires that her dates always ended in thwarted passion. The prayers offered up at night, after each date, did little to make her feel any better. It was all quite frustrating. It felt unnatural. All of her faith in Jesus, and all of her deep gratitude for what he had done for her, and all of the fervent Bible studying—none of it did much to temper the natural urges simmering within her. She was able to make it through high school as "pure" as a young Christian girl should be, more or less. But once she moved away from home and started college, it was just too much to bear. The young men at college were so nice, so attractive, and they were so interested in Geraldine. And she was interested in them. She realized that she simply could not resist any longer.

> I just thought it was crazy that God would demand that you would save yourself until marriage when this was such an insane, crazy desire and it took everything I had not to cave in and go for it.

But finally you...?

> I did.

What happened?

I was 21 and I think I had this realization that, "Let's see—I'm 21. I'm going to be in school for another three or four years and, God, you're expecting me to keep saving myself?" I was just…I pretty much said, "I'm sorry God, I've done the best I could. I can't do this anymore and if you want me back, you can come get me, but I need to go live my life"—because there was so much guilt associated with these thoughts. You know, there were a lot of attractive men around…. There was a guy that I kept running into and I knew that I couldn't keep saying no.

Geraldine started having sex. She enjoyed it and indulged.

There were a number of men in a short succession—I made up for lost time [laughter]. As soon as I stepped over that line, I was like, "Holy crap! I've missed a whole lot here!" and I didn't say no to anyone for a long time…. I think right afterward I felt kind of liberated. I think it was probably, like, there was a little guilt, but mostly like: "Okay!!"

Once Geraldine stopped repressing her sexual desires, she also let go of her deep commitment to God. Soon after becoming sexually active, her Christianity melted away entirely. She hasn't identified as a Christian for about 20 years now and she currently chooses to label herself as an agnostic. She's happily married to a nonreligious Jew, and they have raised their children in a totally secular manner.

The day after I interviewed Geraldine, I interviewed Holly. Although Holly is 20 years younger than Geraldine, her reasons for letting go of the Pentecostal religion that she was raised in were strikingly similar. Holly's upbringing was quite devout; she and her parents attended church every Wednesday night and Sunday morning. They prayed daily, and Holly held a deep love of Jesus and a strong belief in God—until she was 18. That's when her Christianity started to fade. What happened?

Well, honestly, like, I got a boyfriend and fell in love—wanted to—you know—I think it was definitely like the sex thing that you couldn't—I couldn't

be a good Christian and have sex. And I guess my hormones took over and
that became more important.

* * *

Sex was not a significant issue for everyone I interviewed. But for
a notable number of apostates, it was crucial. While they were
religious, they saw their own sexual desires as unclean, unnatural, immoral. They had been raised to feel shame about having
sexual fantasies and to feel guilty about masturbating. And they
were socialized to repress their sexual urges until marriage.
Premarital sex was a despicable affront to God that could adversely
affect the state of one's eternal soul. It was intrinsically sinful
and to be avoided—at all costs. Sociologist Mark Regnerus has
done extensive research among American teenagers, looking specifically at their religiosity in connection with their sex lives and
sexual ethics. In his words:

> The majority of religious interviewees with whom we spoke…could
> articulate nothing more about what their faith has to say about sex than
> a simple no-sex-before-marriage rule. For most of them, this is the sum
> total of Christian teaching on sex.[2]

As Grace, a 42-year-old Catholic-turned-atheist from the Philippines,
conveyed to me:

> *One big thing was that you cannot have sex with just anyone and you cannot*
> *have sex prior to marriage. Sex was like a big deal thing…and I was very*
> *afraid of hell, of course. My mom was very powerful in painting the picture of*
> *hell. She sort of—she has a big voice, very strong personality—so when she*
> *would say you cannot think like that, you cannot have sex before marriage*
> *because you're going to go to hell and you cannot get out of it ever…you're*
> *just going to roast in fire, and that sort of thing.*

Elizabeth is 26 years old. She grew up in Northern California,
near the Oregon border. Her mother was an often-homeless drug

addict and her father was a truck driver who had a habit of disappearing for long stretches at a time, so Elizabeth moved around a lot among aunts, uncles, babysitters, and foster homes. Throughout this difficult childhood, she gained comfort and a sense of security from Christianity. She was a very active churchgoer, solemnly committed to her Christian faith. In addition to daily and nightly prayers and regular Bible reading, she attended Christian summer camps and Christian youth groups all the way through high school. She recalls:

> We were taught that it was a sin to have sex. You don't have sex until you are married and you don't even think in your mind about having sex with someone, because that person is someone else's future husband one day, and you're committing adultery in your mind. . . . In high school I started going to youth group . . . all the boys were Christian—we were all Christian . . . and we all felt really guilty if we made out with them, because it was wrong . . . yeah . . . oral sex was all over tenth grade and—we knew we weren't having sex—so on technicality we weren't doing anything wrong that way. But we would feel guilty and cry about it . . . cry about it to each other, pray about it, and just feel really bad. We had this quote that we would say: "Make sure you have enough room between you for the Holy Spirit to fit." We even wore "pure" bracelets and "love waits" rings.[3]

By the time Elizabeth was a senior in high school, she was an active member of her church's Worship Team, she was teaching Sunday School to kindergarteners, and she was president of her high school's Christian Club. She took her faith so seriously—and tried so hard to resist sexual feelings and activities—that she didn't go to her senior prom, for fear that it would be too difficult to resist temptation. For Elizabeth, and many of the people whom I interviewed, grappling with sexual urges was the "ultimate spiritual battle" in their young lives. It seemed to be the most important way to be worthy in the eyes of God. But eventually, for some, the desire became too compelling, contributing to their apostasy.

Recall Ed, who was profiled in the first chapter of this book. As he explained,

> *My religion definitely affected me. I waited a long time. I waited until I was almost 18, which to me seems like a really long time, especially since I probably wanted to since I was 15 or something....I waited. I really waited....I thought I was going to wait until I was married.*

Ed had many girlfriends during his high school years, and he basically did "everything but" with them. But just before his eighteenth birthday, he lost his virginity, along with his faith:

> *It happened one night, sort of by accident.*

Did you have protection?

> *No, not at all. I was like 17 and had this girlfriend—a senior in high school. It was not romantic or beautiful or anything, but it just... we just got taken by the moment....So I was starting to let go of things already at this point—so I think I was just—weakening to Christianity and gave in, you know.*

Did you feel any guilt afterwards, personally?

> *Not that much....I only felt bad for not feeling bad, you know what I mean?*

For Ed, and also for Geraldine, the choice to engage in premarital sex was liberating and was not riddled with too much guilt or self-loathing. But for other apostates, the feelings of shame and immorality that had for so long been associated with sex were hard to shake, and some experienced intense guilt for quite some time. Jayme is 37 years old. She grew up in Illinois and was raised in a prayerful Protestant home. She struggled with her sexual desires throughout her teenage years, and after she indulged, she felt guilty and began questioning of her faith:

I experimented a lot—especially in my church youth group—with a lot of things. But not sex. Not actual sex. And that was because it was kind of "everything but."...I had a boyfriend and I think I was a sophomore in high school and he was a senior. He just couldn't get why I wouldn't have sex. But I held firm...mostly—I probably said something along the lines of "I don't believe it's right"...maybe. But...um-m-m...he and I finally did have pre-marital sex a while later and I struggled with that for a long time...feeling like, "Oh, I'm not supposed to be doing this but I want to do this." You know, I had one other long-term boyfriend that I was actually engaged to and I think all throughout our four-year relationship, I think I would feel guilty almost every time. And this is still after college....So that was during that prime time when I was grappling with am I a Christian? What do I believe? But I still felt guilty...guilty, guilty.

Once a strong Christian, Jayme is now an agnostic. And it took her many years to stop feeling shameful or guilty after having sex, even with her husband—a common fate for women from similar backgrounds.[4]

Maxine, age 20, is a senior in college and a former nondenominational Christian. She recalls the heavy feelings of guilt that accompanied her first sexual experiences:

I started hanging out with this guy, and we started dating, and then—like that was the first time I had ever went down on a guy. And I remember being SO guilty about it...it was, like, such a deep guilt—like, I had let down my future husband, I had let down God....I would just like cry and cry and cry...letting God down...it was a very heavy, heavy thing.

Brian is 25 years old and works as a junior high school teacher in Nevada. Raised a Catholic, today he is nonreligious. Early sexual activity coincided with his loss of faith:

Premarital sex was a big issue, too. Because you're a young, adolescent teen wanting to get some ass, you know? And you've got that guilt up in your mind....But I'd go out with girls and make out...like, sex is natural...but, you know, that first girlfriend I had when I was a sophomore, I was just paranoid... you know: "Do I need to go to confession?" There were a couple of times my freshman and sophomore year they almost sucked me back in to go to that b.s.—I got to the door and I was, like, this is stupid. And I left.

*   *   *

If there is any one form of human interaction that is "natural," surely it is sex. Sexual urges and desires lay at the core of our biological and psychological being. We are neurologically wired for it, emotionally dependent on it, and physiologically designed for it. And it feels good. Granted, there is a range of just how strong or central a role sex plays in various people's lives. For some individuals, sexual urges may be weak or minimal, while for others, they are downright all-powerful. Most of us probably fall somewhere in between. And the variety of human sexual expressions and experiences is fascinatingly varied and diverse. But, remarkably, what is not so varied or diverse is the standard, narrow approach that most dominant religions take concerning sex and sexuality. Simply put: sex as experienced between married heterosexual couples is good, while all other forms of human sexual expression are bad. While there are some variations on this theme, it is essentially the same in almost all Western religions—certainly within traditional forms of Judaism, Christianity, and Islam. As the popular radio and television talk show host Laura Schlessinger has more or less accurately summed up: "Holy sex is between a husband and wife.... Unholy sex is everything else."[5] And it is just this narrow and essentially unrealistic conception of human sexuality that many apostates simply cannot abide. For them, sex prior to or outside of heterosexual marriage is not only inevitable but something to be celebrated. And they harbor varying degrees of resentment toward those, be they parents or preachers, who taught them otherwise. Their rejection of religion was intimately linked to the pain they experienced during their prolonged attempts to suppress their natural sexual urges.

It should come as no surprise that studies consistently find that secular people are markedly less fearful or guilt-ridden about sex than religious people, and they are more likely to enjoy a wider variety of sexual practices. In terms of attitudes about sex, secular men and women are less likely than religious people to condemn masturbation, less likely to feel guilty after masturbating or having sex, less likely to condemn nontraditional sexual behaviors in general, and much less likely to condemn homosexuality, specifically. Secular people are more likely to engage in and enjoy oral sex, with secular women being much more likely than religious women to receive oral sex. Additionally, secular individuals are more likely to engage in premarital sex and to engage in anal sex. They have sex more often and for longer periods of time, and they are more likely to have more sexual partners.[6] And yet, on top of all this, secular men and women engage in safer sex than religious men and women,[7] and religious teenagers are significantly less knowledgeable about sex and safe-sex practices than secular teenagers.[8] Perhaps this is all related to the recent finding that religious parents are markedly less comfortable talking about sex and birth control with their teenagers than are secular parents,[9] which in turn helps explain the fact that when religiously motivated abstinence-pledgers eventually do have sex, they usually do so without the use of contraception, thereby increasing the risk of STDs, not to mention pregnancy. Most of the men and women I talked to were so fearful of sex and felt such shame about it, that when they did eventually engage in it, they were ill-prepared, and didn't use condoms. And the "abstinence only" sexual education some received wasn't helpful, to say the least.[10]

*   *   *

When honest information about sex is denied and instead replaced with unhelpful silence at best, or fear-inducing condemnation at worst, grappling with sexual desire can be a treacherous and painful process. When teenagers are taught next to nothing about sex—other than that it is sinful and is to be avoided before marriage—their premarital sexual encounters are likely to be less safe and will be experienced with varying degrees of fear and anxiety. Apostates' testimony reveals as much. So do national and international statistics, which show that it is in the least religious democracies on earth that teen pregnancy and STD rates are the lowest, while it is among the most religious democracies on earth that teen pregnancy and STD rates are the highest. The same holds true within the United States; we find the highest rates of teen pregnancy and STDs in those states that are the most religious in terms of both belief and practice. One study found that in Lubbock, Texas, in the years after religious-mandated "abstinence sex education" was instituted throughout the school system in 1995, rates of gonorrhea increased to double the national average, and the teen pregnancy rate is now the highest in the state.[11]

Obviously, guilt or anxiety around sex does not necessarily cause apostasy in and of itself. After all, most children who are raised to feel guilt and shame about sex do not go on to reject religion. But religious teachings about sex can—for a distinct minority of men and women—create negative emotional outcomes that, when colluding with other factors, result in an eventual loss of faith and rejection of religion.

*   *   *

An obvious question arises: Why don't people just switch religions? Surely there are many religions with more open, liberal approaches to human sexuality. Perhaps some of the people I interviewed would be very happy in a Unitarian Universalist congregation, a Quaker meeting, a mainline liberal Protestant church, or a Reconstructionist synagogue. And as for homosexuals specifically, surely there are a number of religious communities that are accepting and welcoming. Rather than reject religion entirely, why don't they switch to a milder or less objectionable religious denomination?

To begin with, the majority of people that I interviewed became atheists or strong agnostics as the endpoint of their apostasy.

Simply put: they lost their faith—not only in their given religion, but in God. So they did not feel compelled to seek out a religious denomination or congregation more "in line" with their theology. Their theology had evaporated. By way of analogy: a person who has become a vegetarian doesn't seek out a more palatable kind of meat to eat—he or she has rejected flesh altogether and is happy with that choice. So it goes with most apostates—they are just not interested in religion anymore; they're content in their acquired secularity. Furthermore, most people who walk away from their religion—even if they happen to maintain a kernel of spirituality or mystical beliefs—do not feel the need to look for a replacement of the religion they have rejected. They don't feel motivated to research the various religious options available in their community in order to select a new or better religion that might be more personally comfortable or acceptable. While many Americans do indeed "shop around" for a religion or congregation that matches their personal tastes, not all Americans do so. Most apostates have simply been soured.

When Brian gave up Catholicism, he did not become an outright atheist. He still does believe there is "something" out there, and he thinks that some sort of divine intervention saved his brother from a harrowing bike accident. He is what I referred to earlier as a "shallow" apostate. I asked him why he doesn't try to find a new religion, one perhaps more in line with his worldview. He replied,

> When I was a junior or senior in high school, I took a world religions class and studied Hinduism, Judaism, Buddhism, Islam, Christianity. . . . I realized that all of these religions had things that I disagreed with—whether it was issues with these religions accepting other religions, accepting different sexuality—homosexuality in particular—and/or premarital sex. Seeing as though these were the biggest reasons for me not to be a part of the Catholic Church, I couldn't see myself being a part of these other religions that I studied. . . . I also came to the realization that I have a problem with many religions because of the lack of respect or lack of acceptance of women in religions—women not being held in as high regard as men—male superiority, maybe. This was a big

issue for me. . . . To sum it all up simply, most religions that I have studied don't value the same thing that I value—respect for ALL cultures, sexuality, gender, and ethnicity. . . . Although I find value—and I respect some or most of what the other religions practice and preach, I don't want to associate myself with a religion or denomination unless I agree with it 100% because I don't want to be a hypocrite or liar. I just want to be truthful about who I am and what I am about, and that is respect for everybody.

Is there a church or denomination out there that holds the same values that Brian has? Perhaps. But clearly Brian just isn't interested in searching it out.

6

✧

Others

By the time William Lobdell was in his late twenties, his life was "screwed up." His marriage to his high school sweetheart was a mess, the girlfriend he was seeing on the side was pregnant, and his career was going nowhere. He was depressed and desperate. A friend told him that what he needed in his life was God. So he decided to give it a shot. One night, at a Christian retreat in the mountains, he committed his life to Jesus, accepting Him into his heart as his personal savior. And his life began to improve. Christianity was just the self-help program he needed. He divorced his first wife and married his pregnant girlfriend. They had more kids together. And his career took off: he became a full-time reporter for the *Los Angeles Times*, covering the religion beat. William spent the next several years deepening his love of Jesus through prayer, faith, tithing, and worship. He was a happy and inspired born-again Christian, basking in the warm glow of God's grace. In his column, he reported on the inspirational, altruistic, and holy endeavors of people of faith—men and women who opened up their homes to the homeless, fed the hungry and destitute, and worked to make the world a better place through their piety, mercy, and goodwill.[1]

And then, in the early 1990s, he stumbled onto some news stories related to religion that weren't so savory. William started investigating some pretty hard-core cases of violent sexual abuse perpetrated by Catholic priests. He met many of the victims. He attended their group therapy sessions. He spoke with their parents. He learned about the pernicious degree to which the higher-ups in the Catholic Church had—for decades–shamefully shielded these pedophile priests from prosecution, hiding their crimes from the public, lying about their past abuses, and reassigning them to new parishes in different parts of the country where their predatory predilections were unleashed upon new victims. One official report from 2004 found that, since the 1950s, 4,392 priests had sexually abused as many as 10,000 minors. Only 2% had ever done time in prison. To add insult to injury, the Catholic Church spurned and vilified the victims. As William concluded from his extensive investigations, "The real story wasn't about the molesting priests, but rather the bishops who covered up for them and caused thousands of additional children to be sodomized, orally copulated, raped, and masturbated."[2] The more he learned about the extent of Catholic priest abuse and the concomitant coverup, the greater William's shock and dismay became. And then he began reporting on various manifestations of malfeasance within Protestant circles. He followed the likes of charismatic faith-healer-millionaire Benny Hinn, who promises endless streams of poor, suffering people that he'll heal their cancer or diabetes or multiple sclerosis if they just give him all their money. The more William began witnessing unethical Christian scams like this within the Evangelical community, the greater his distaste for religion became. Suddenly, he found himself in the company of something perhaps quieter than a barking dog, but just as persistent: doubt.

Of course, he knew that he shouldn't interpret the misdeeds of various corrupt religious people as evidence that there is no God. Just because some televangelist is a swindler doesn't mean that Jesus didn't die for our sins. Just because thousands of priests have abused thousands of kids doesn't mean that the Bible isn't divine. After all, humans are sinful. This line of thinking sustained William's faith for several years. But it eventually trickled away. Gnawing doubts—sparked by his investigations into the unethical actions of religious people—were joined by new ones. He started researching Christianity, learning about its history, its sources, its contradictions. He began looking at the Bible with a skeptical, critical eye, rather than just accepting it as God's word. He studied other religions like Scientology and Mormonism, and he realized that what he believed as a Christian was just as strange and just as evidenceless as what they believed.

William didn't like the idea of becoming an atheist, and he resisted that possibility for many years. But finally, after much inner turmoil, and quite a few hours staring up at the ceiling at night, that's what happened. As he recalls, "As deeply as I missed my faith, as hard as I tried to keep it, my head could not command my gut. I know now that it was wishful thinking, not truth. I just didn't believe in God anymore, despite my best attempts to hold on to my beliefs."[3]

While there were many factors that contributed to William's loss of faith, the initial and perhaps most significant cause was his learning about the extensive crimes of religious people. His discovery that God's followers can be wicked and deceitful, that religious institutions can be wracked with hypocrisy and corruption, and that religious people do not lead lives that are any more moral or ethical than secular people, caused him to eventually reject his religion.

THE MALFEASANCE OF OTHERS

One of the main reasons many apostates cite as to why they eventually rejected their religion was that someone within their religious circle—often a clergyman—was hypocritical, unkind, or immoral. And this behavior came as such a shock that it spawned their eventual apostasy.

Juan provides an excellent example. Juan was born in Mexico, but he immigrated with his grandparents to a small farming town in New Mexico when he was six years old. They were poor, they were hard-working, they were strong Catholics, and Juan was raised accordingly. He vividly remembers the little altar his grandmother erected in their home, featuring Saint Martin de Porres, known for his tireless work on behalf of the poor, the sick, and the orphaned. This saint was very important to Juan's grandmother:

> She would always say, "Well, here was this saint and he would give up every-thing he had to work and organize the poor so that they would have a better life."

Juan was a devoted believer growing up. He served as an altar boy in their local parish, and his faith was strong.

> I was so much into it—into religion . . . that I really believed that if you went to confession and you confessed your sins, then you received the host, that when you walked out of that church, if a car hit you, you'd go straight to heaven. So you almost got to the point where you literally say to yourself in the back of your mind, "Why, I sort of hope that happens to me, because I'll go straight to heaven." But you knew that you couldn't willingly do that because then you'd go to hell. So I really believed that.

Directly influenced by his grandmother's devotion to Saint Martin de Porres, Juan became a community organizer and social activist, fighting for the rights of poor people throughout the Southwest, particularly migrant farm workers. He worked with indigenous communities, helping the Native Americans in their struggles. He worked with unions and labor organizations, eventually occupying a significant position within Cesar Chavez's National Farm Workers Association, which became the United Farm Workers. He saw his work with the poor as a logical extension of his faith. But then, something happened that significantly soured Juan's religious identification. It involved the misfortunes of some Kickapoo Indians, and the failure of a Catholic priest and his congregation to act in a Christ-like manner.

There was a group of Kickapoo Indians who were living in horse stalls in the area of Brighton, Colorado. This farmer had been keeping them there in really bad conditions. We just thought that was terrible. So we were able to go and organize them and then pull them out of those horse stalls. Then we set up a tent city next to a river. So we had children, we had all kinds of families. Community people donated tents and beds and all kinds of things. Well, one night... I was staying at my grandmother's house and the phone rings. I pick up the phone at 3:00 in the morning. Someone is calling me: "You've got to get over here." It was raining really hard, and he said a flood has just hit the river.... So when I got there, sure enough, you know, I could see the people just soaking wet—mothers holding children with water up to their knees. They really didn't know where to go or what to do. And we didn't know what to do. So the only thing we can think of is we've got to go to the church. That was our first thought because the church had always supported—and that's what they should do. So we went and knocked on the priest's door in Brighton. This priest... was really upset that we even woke him up so late at night. We told him what had happened and that the Kickapoo Indians are out there and they need a place to stay and could the church have them stay just one night? His response was, "Well, the only place that they could possibly stay would be in the basement, but we just put in a new red rug there and I don't think the board would really like that, so I'm going to have to say no." So I argued with him and said, what do you mean? You have an entire room down there where they could sleep and we're only asking for one night. He refused and literally closed the door on us. So...that morning at 11:00 a.m., I and others went to the Board...because we still didn't have a place.... We went to the Board to ask them if they could use the basement for the next night because we didn't have anywhere else. So the Board discussed it, and I just remember that discussion. It had no spiritual content, no loving content, it was just this material rug, this room—and they voted no. I just couldn't believe it. I, at that point, said you know if Jesus Christ came here without any shoes and he'd been out in the desert and asked you for a place to stay, all of you would turn him down. Shame on you. I walked out of there just *totally upset and totally angry at the whole church structure.... That began a period of time where I just did not go to mass. I didn't go to confession. I didn't go to communion. I began to question the whole validity of the church. Then I began to see, I guess, the other side of the church that maybe I just hadn't seen. I saw priests who were never out in the community, but in their offices and asking for money passed on Sunday. Seeing these huge churches that were built with this ... I just began to see that part and I began to study and see that the church was the largest landowner in the world and it wasn't just a church that was loving and caring. That in some places there were priests who were fighting right alongside the governments against the poor. And I really began to question whether, you know, the way the Bible or the way the church described the Father, the Son, and the Holy Ghost. I began to question all of that.... So having that moment when this Board votes the way they do and turn away these poor people—it just had a tremendous effect on me.*

Juan never went back to church, and he raised his two sons without any religion at all. Today he is a 62-year-old agnostic.

Like Juan, Chuck—who is 36 years old and works in a library—was very religious growing up. For years he was enmeshed in the communal vitality and spiritual enthusiasm of his Assemblies of God congregation, and as he grew older, he internalized the beliefs and practices of this brand of Pentecostal Christianity, speaking in tongues on a regular basis, being "slain the spirit" at revivals, praying frequently, and studying the Bible—which he was taught was the direct word of God. For Chuck, the presence of the Lord in his life was joyous and visceral, "as obvious as the sun rising." But then his pastor did something quite upsetting, and Chuck's taste for religion was irrevocably soured.

I started playing Dungeons and Dragons with some friends of mine. I really loved that stuff. For a young mind, it's really engaging stuff, it's really fascinating. Well, when I was 13, this pastor—the youth pastor—he came—see ... my mom was worried. She saw this book "Deities and Demigods." She was freaked out about it because it's a book that lists all these gods and their various attributes and so forth. She had heard through the Christian community—at the time especially, there was that Satanic panic going on—you know, where like everything was Satanic and Satan was behind every manifestation of pop culture and, you know. So definitely D & D was at the top of the list....

And when I was 13, our pastor came to my house and he took all my D&D books, which was a major investment for a young kid [laughs]. All my allowance money went into those books. Plus it was my social identity outside of church. So, you know, I was in a group of other kids who all were into this thing. So he had all the books—my mom had given them to him—and he took me on a ride in his Volkswagen bug...and he started telling me how these things are evil and they are a tool of Satan. I remember arguing with him, and I remember realizing at some point that he's going to take my fucking books—because he had them all back there. I told him at one point that you're not going to take those books. I remember getting—almost fighting—like I was ready to hit him. I was really upset. He did take my books. He said he was going to burn them. I don't know what he did with them, but they disappeared. He dropped me back off at home and I was devastated. I mean, really...so at that time I left the church....I remember me telling my mom, "Because you've done this to me, I will never, ever go to that church again."

In the wake of this event, Chuck got a hold of his deceased father's dusty copy of *Why I Am Not a Christian* by Bertrand Russell, and that sealed the deal. Today he describes himself as an "absolute nonbeliever."

For one final example, recall Jayme. Her apostasy had several sources, but one of the earliest was the malfeasance of the youth pastor at her church:

Our youth pastor—we all revered him. Then I come to find out—maybe a year or two after my little posse graduated—that he cheated on his wife and got kicked out of the church. To my young mind, you know, Christians don't do that, you know? Things like that...they put a dent in how you respect the belief system. Because obviously the people in it weren't respecting it...things like that contributed to my questioning.

OTHER PEOPLE, OTHER RELIGIONS

While apostasy can often be spurred by the malfeasance of others—in many cases, malfeasance has nothing to do with it. Just meeting, getting to know, or learning about other people who have other religious beliefs, or secular worldviews, can have a corrosive effect on a person's own religious convictions. The case of Daniel Everett, a linguistics professor at Illinois State University, provides a compelling example.[4]

Back in the 1970s, Daniel went deep into the Amazon rain forest with his wife and three small children, traveling into one of the most remote regions of the South American jungle—a place without running water, electricity, or phone lines. No stores, no roads, no radios, no doctors. It was a region of the Amazon so deep, wild, and isolated that the small group of indigenous people that live there speak a language unlike any other spoken on earth. His initial reason for going to live among these natives of the Amazon—know as the Pirahãs—was to convert them to Christianity. As a committed missionary (and budding linguist) he lived among them, on and off, for over 30 years. But the Pirahãs had no interest in Daniel's Bible, his Savior, or his God; he never did get them to accept Jesus Christ. Although their unyielding resistance to Christianity was hard for Daniel to accept, he eventually came to terms with it. And the more he learned about and understood Pirahã culture—their outlook, their heritage, their mentality—the greater his appreciation and respect for them became. Eventually, after living among the Pirahãs for so many years, developing deep friendships and extensive bonds, and being exposed to their morals and values, Daniel experienced a depletion of his own Christian zeal. As he explains in his fascinating book *Don't Sleep, There Are Snakes*:

All the doctrines and faith I had held dear were a glaring irrelevancy in this culture. They were superstition to the Pirahãs. And they began to seem more and more like superstition to me....I began to seriously question the nature of faith, the act of believing in something unseen.... There was no sense of sin among the Pirahãs, no need to "fix" mankind or even themselves. There was acceptance for things the way they are, by and large. No fear of death. Their faith was in themselves....So, sometime in the late 1980s, I came to admit to myself alone that I no longer believed in any article of faith or in anything supernatural. I was a closet atheist.[5]

Of course, none of the apostates that I interviewed ever went to the Amazon rain forest in order to unexpectedly have their faith evaporate. But they did have similar experiences as Daniel Everett did—though certainly on a much smaller, less dramatic scale—in which their interacting with and/or learning about other people, other cultures, and other religions created a crisis of faith that led eventually to apostasy.

Lily is from a midsized city in Massachusetts. Her mother was a nurse and her father drove a forklift. They were active and believing nondenominational Christians who went to church every Sunday, and most Wednesdays as well. Lily recalls that faith, prayer, and belief in God permeated her youth. In fact, through her teenage years, she had never even imagined the possibility that there could not be a God. But things changed. Lily eventually became a nonbeliever. Today, she rarely thinks or cares about religious matters at all.

When I was 18 I studied abroad in Estonia for a year. And I met people— these modern people who had been—really didn't even know how to pronounce "Jesus." And they weren't really sure of his name! You know, having grown up in the Soviet Union and Christianity not being a part of their lives, it was just like—whooo!—there are living, breathing people out there that don't even have any religious identification. It was really eye opening for me. . . . Then there was another student from Denmark who was hosted in my village as well, and in talking with her about this—she was raised in a secular home and her parents were atheists, so me being religious was a very interesting concept for her. Because I was intelligent and educated, yet religious. And her not being religious—for me—was another concept—because she was intelligent and nice and educated, yet not religious. So it opened up a whole lot of conversations where we were able to learn a lot about what the other side was like. We had a very close relationship, so we were able to ask a lot of questions. . . . I think it contributed greatly to my agnosticism . . . When I came back when I was 19 I think I did try to go to church on my own a couple of times, but it just never quite . . . didn't quite set right with me. . . . It felt like I had to put a lot of effort into belief. . . . I don't know if that's what belief is supposed to feel like—or faith is supposed to feel like—but you have to make

an effort to believe. Then I just kind of didn't really believe any more. It wasn't
a great moment, or moment of clarity. It was . . . I just wasn't really able to
believe any more.

Coming from a pious home in the United States, which is perhaps the most religious democracy in the Western world,
Estonian secularity was a true culture shock to Lily. Estonia is
actually one of the least religious countries in the world; according
to a 2005 study, only 16% of Estonians believe in God—among
the lowest levels of theism ever recorded by social science. It was
quite an adjustment for Lily to live in such a secular society. And
it clearly had a secularizing effect on her. To live among "normal"
people—people who go about their daily lives, studying, working,
loving, etc., and yet don't ever think about Jesus much and don't
believe in God—eventually caused Lily to see the world differently, to recognize that her own religiosity was clearly the result
of how, where, and by whom she was raised rather then incon-
trovertible divine truth. Finally, she no longer believed in
Christianity at all.[6]

Mercedes didn't leave the United States. Rather, she came
here. And that move started her on the road to apostasy. At age
47, Mercedes isn't an atheist. She considers herself "spiritual,"
maintaining that there are meaningful truths to be found in
many religions, particularly Buddhism. But she is certainly no
longer the strong, believing Catholic she once was. She's been
"detached from her faith," as she put it, for many years. She
grew up on a small city in central Mexico, where Catholicism
permeated all aspects of life. But after she moved to the United
States, her Catholicism evaporated:

Back in Mexico, when I was there, Catholicism was just not—it was my
culture, it was just my life. So it was something inseparable, completely. I
could not even dream of questioning my religion. It was just very strong . . . the
idea of having another religion was attached to the devil or you're going to be
sick, you're going to die if you do something else. So nobody really ever ques-
tioned those things. Probably, in part related to my moving to this country—

and reading and learning about other cultures and learning about other religions—and then I started, in a way, questioning issues about my own faith...I started to really—questioning.

Nathan didn't go to another country—but he did go to a Christian college where he encountered a group of people with strong religious beliefs somewhat different from his own. Just getting to know these people had a corrosive effect on his faith. There he was, a devout Pentecostal, and while studying for his master's degree, he came upon a group of Calvinists. This interaction would force Nathan to start asking some tough questions:

Trinity was the place that I probably would say that I really, really began to question Christianity. Because they had a lot of Calvinists. Up until that point, I hadn't had much interaction with Calvinists. I didn't even really think that they existed....My engagement with the Calvinists probably was the most important aspect of me really challenging Christianity, because their view—to me—was so bizarre. The idea that God would create people basically to destroy. The fact that there was this vibrant Christian community of people who wrote the best books and who—the greatest Christian scholars had this kind of perspective, made me really seriously think...If God was engaging humanity, would God allow a vibrant Christian community to believe this? Then I also thought, if these people were so deceived at believing this crazy worldview, then maybe I'm just as susceptible.

Many other apostates described their experience of learning about other religions, especially while in college, as having a secularizing effect. Again, from Jayme:

If I had to pinpoint a turning point...it might have been my sophomore year—I was taking two classes side by side. One was a world religions class and I just learned so much. It's like, well—there's all these different religions. Why and how—and how dare—Christians say we are it, the way, the truth, the light, we're the only way to go, everything else you're damned. I just...suddenly that did not compute anymore. It just didn't compute....I think it was studying Gandhi that really shifted me. Because again, he's not a Christian,

and look at the good in the world that he did and look at his values and how
he treated people. I just could no longer say Christianity had the
answers...which was very scary to me to think along those lines.

For many other men and women I interviewed, learning about
other religions had a secularizing effect. So, too, did living in a
foreign culture and dwelling among people who held markedly
different ways of looking at the world. The secularizing effect of
these phenomena manifests itself in three ways. First, by learning
about or becoming acquainted with other people who hold different religious beliefs, one is forced to contemplate the following
question: if *they* can believe *that*, then why do I believe *this*?
Admittedly, for most believers, this question isn't too vexing:
they believe that because they are duped, misguided, or ignorant,
and I believe this because it is true. But for a minority of believers,
that answer isn't satisfying. It is too pat, too pithy, too simplistic.
They reckon that if other people can be convinced of vastly different religious beliefs—which when viewed from the outside seem
mistaken or bizarre—then maybe someone else could view their
own religious beliefs in a similar fashion. And who is to say who
is right? And how can they know? Such questions can, in certain
circumstances, pull the rug of certainty out from under one's
feet. Second, by learning about other religions, particularly the
good there within (recall Jayme's study of Gandhi), one's worldview expands. It becomes more difficult to sustain a belief in
one's own religious supremacy when faced with the goodness to
be found outside of that tradition. So long as one stays within
one's own religious waters, it is easy to contently float along,
assuming that one's religion possesses superior truth. But when
one starts to sample other waters, or even just read about them,
such certainty can wither. Finally, living in a different culture—
like Estonia—can undermine, or at least challenge, one's personal
assumptions. When we go and live in a different culture, many of
the things that we had always taken for granted as being obvious
or true or real are suddenly called into question. Religion sometimes falls into this category. In the case of Lily, it wasn't that

most Estonians held a firm conviction in a different religion, but rather, they didn't hold any firm religious convictions at all. At first, this fact confounded her. But eventually, it ended up corroding her own faith. Being closely acquainted with other cultures—especially those that practice a different religion or no religion at all—can have that effect. It thus makes perfect sense that out of all academic disciplines, social scientists—especially anthropologists—maintain the highest rates of atheism and secularity.[7]

LILY'S INSIGHT

Recall something Lily said during her interview:

You have to make an effort to believe.

This simple sentiment illuminates a great deal—not only about apostasy but about religiosity. With this single sentence, Lily has captured a critical piece of the essence of religious belief: it is often based on will, choice, *effort*. There is, however, one crucial exception to all of this, which is the religiosity of children. Most children do not make a concerted effort to believe in certain religious teachings. Most kids will believe anything they are told, most of the time—especially if it comes from people they know and love. As psychologist Michael Argyle has argued, "Children readily take to religion, and accept whatever they are told without difficulty."[8] The religiosity of children stems largely from their socialization; they generally believe whatever their parents or primary caregivers tell them to believe. But this form of uncritical religious acceptance does not last forever. As children grow older, as their minds mature, they eventually start to wonder about and reflect upon their religious beliefs. Three possible outcomes result. They may maintain an affiliation and commitment to the religious tradition they were raised in because it provides them with a sense of community, heritage, tradition, and/or family bonding, and they just let the questionable or opaque beliefs of their religion cruise along for the ride, never outright rejecting them, but also not obsessing about them too much. Or they may decide to fully believe what they have been taught to believe—they come to personally accept the beliefs of their religion as meaningful, true, and valid—a decision that will entail various degrees of willful effort. Finally, they may find that the effort to believe is too heavy a burden to bear, that they don't have the will or the desire to believe what they were once taught, and that, in the end, they just don't buy it.

Faith is willed. It is deliberate. Admittedly, in some circumstances, the effort to believe religious teachings is quite minimal, such as when one is regularly surrounded by like-minded believers and if one is supported in one's beliefs by one's family and friends, or if one dwells in a culture predominated by one single religious worldview.[9] As Steve Bruce has put it, "With the right social support and in the right social context, the threat to [religious] beliefs from some specific counter-propositions can be neutralized."[10] Peter Berger emphasizes what he calls "plausibility structures" as being central to religion's existence; plausibility structures are specific social processes, dynamics, or interactions within a group of people sharing a common view and understanding of the world.[11] A solid, pervasive, and monopolistic plausibility structure allows personal religious beliefs to have a "taken-for-granted" quality—a naturalness that renders acceptance of them quite easy and matter of fact. But in other social circumstances in which plausibility structures are weak, diverse, or threatened, the effort to believe can become harder, heavier, and more onerous. Such circumstances can make believing so difficult that people drop the load altogether, leaving religion by the side of the road. This final outcome—the rejection of religious belief—can be caused in part by witnessing or experiencing the malfeasance of religious associates or leaders, or by familiarity with other people, other cultures, or other religions. Such factors make the effort to believe harder, more personally onerous.

If religious belief was not based on willful effort, then these factors wouldn't pose a threat to religiosity. So what if there are some crooked or unethical religious people out there? That, in and of itself, should not cause one to lose faith in God. So what if there are other religions out there teaching other tenets? Or other cultures out there with different or secular worldviews? Why would a knowledge of or familiarity with such differences render one's religion moot? The answer is clear: belief in God isn't easy. The belief that Jesus shed his blood to save us from hell, or that Muhammad rode a flying white horse through the sky, or that one's religion is uniquely valid, requires effort. Clearly, for a minority of people, certain social circumstances can make the effort too much to bear.

* * *

Earlier, I noted an apparent paradox. Personal misfortune can often lead to apostasy, but societal misfortune is correlated with overall increased religiosity. However, there is one factor—the malfeasance of others—that does seem to play a similarly secularizing role at both micro and macro levels. When religious people in one's immediate circle behave unethically, this malfeasance can be a contributing cause of apostasy at the individual level. And such malfeasance—if widespread, dramatic, and well publicized—may contribute toward secularization at the macro, societal level as well. As we know, irreligion is on the rise in America. More Americans are self-identifying as atheists and agnostics than ever before. Sociologist Barry Kosmin's research reveals that the irreligious population in the United States is currently growing by 750,000 people a year. Simultaneously, the percentage of Americans claiming to be Christian has dropped from 86% in 1990 down to 76% in 2008. While American society is certainly quite far from losing its religion, a modicum of secularization has definitely occurred. And it is very possible that malfeasance on the part of the religious has been at least one of the contributing components to this current rise of irreligion in the United States. Both the Catholic Church child-molestation scandal and the radical Islamic terrorist attacks of September 11th probably caused some Americans to question religion, and maybe even choose to reject their own.[12]

7

⌖

Jail, Food Stamps, and Atheism

Of the 87 people interviewed, I was perhaps most surprised and intrigued by Rita and Nancy—two individuals I would have never expected to reject religion.

For starters, they're both women. And if there's one clear pattern when it comes to humans and religion, it is that women are, on average, more religious than men. This pattern holds true at all age levels, among all races and ethnicities, in all denominations, and in all countries, as has been consistently borne out in numerous studies on every measure of religiosity the world over. The converse of this, obviously, is that very few women are secular. For example, sociologist Ariela Keysar reports that men make up 58% of Americans who claim to be nonreligious, 70% who identify as atheist, and 75% who identify as agnostic.[1]

In addition, both Nancy and Rita have been relatively poor for most of their lives. When I first met Rita, she was a single mother of two small kids, and she had just ended a short stint working at Blockbuster Video. For much of the last few years, she's just barely managed to get by on food stamps. I recall one time when I ran into her and asked her how she was doing, she told me—with an air of tired resignation—that she had just run out of food stamps the previous day, and was only able to purchase some mac-and-cheese by raiding her three-year-old daughter's piggy bank. As for Nancy, she had been working as a waitress at Marie Callender's for several years. Her boyfriend is a part-time truck driver and was often unemployed. Both Rita and Nancy have been without health insurance for as long as they can remember. I mention all of this because these factors make them more likely to be religious. Although there are some exceptions (depending on what specific measures one takes into account), many studies show that there is a direct correlation between class standing and religious faith, with poorer people being more likely to hold strong religious beliefs than wealthier people, on average. For a specific example within the United States, a recent *New York Times* national survey found that 79% of poor Americans feel that it is "very important" to have faith in God, but only 54% of wealthy Americans feel the same.[2]

I should also mention that higher education hasn't been a big part of Nancy's and Rita's lives either. None of their parents attended college. And both of these women—at least when I first met them—hadn't gotten too far with their own educations. This is yet another factor that would cause one to expect them to be religious. There is a clear correlation between educational attainment and religiosity—the less education a person has, the more likely he or she will be a strong believer.[3]

In sum, being female, lower- or working-class, without a college degree, and American is a veritable recipe for being religious, at least according to the dictates of sociological averages. But sociological averages are just that—averages. There are plenty of exceptions, like Rita and Nancy. However, having said that, Rita and Nancy actually were quite religious for much of their lives. They were both Bible-believing Christians. But by the time I met them, they were done with the Bible, done with Christianity, and done with religion. They had let go of God, walked away from church, replaced prayer with self-motivation, and embraced a fully secular orientation.

Today, Rita describes herself like this:

I'm an atheist. A strong atheist. I don't believe in any kind of supernatural anything. . . . I think that there's coincidences that happen. . . . I just think that things just happen sometimes and maybe we don't know why, but it's not anything to do with God or Jesus or anything like that.

And here is how Nancy describes herself:

I would probably say I'm an atheist. . . . I argue with my next-door neighbor all the time because she apparently is praying for me, or something . . . one day she asked me about God or believing in God. I said it's a crock of shit, you know?

*   *   *

"I don't know how many times I went to jail," Nancy said to me, midway through our interview. She is now 32 years old. When she was 16, she moved out of her mother's apartment and lived with a friend, then with various boyfriends, who were usually older than her by several years. She dropped out of school, started getting high a lot, and began committing crimes—everything from driving under the influence (without a license), to petty theft, to drug-related crimes, to minor burglaries, to violating probation. Her stay behind bars was usually no more than a night or two, though occasionally longer: a week here, two weeks there. She'd party hard with friends and/or boyfriends—drinking and getting wasted on drugs—then at some point she'd commit some crime, get arrested, go to jail—and then while she was in jail she'd make a promise to herself and to God that she's stay clean and sober, and try to live a better life. But then she'd get out of jail and the cycle would start all over again. She was young and relatively rudderless.

During her early childhood, Nancy's family was quite poor. Her father was an alcoholic who had trouble holding down a job. They often went without dinner, and she could not ever recall her mother entering the house with bags full of groceries. Fortunately, charitable people from a nearby Mormon church occasionally brought them food and clothes. But when Nancy was around 4 or 5, her father's situation improved—he got sober through

Alcoholics Anonymous, found God, and started to turn his life around. That's when he started taking Nancy to church. But Nancy's mother, who was also an alcoholic, didn't get sober and didn't find God. She resented her husband's change. Their relationship soured. They fought. They divorced. Nancy lived mostly with her mother, but she spent her weekends with her father— and they always went to church.

> *I loved it.... Church was always good. We always did fun things. I mean, going to people's houses, swimming, and that kind of stuff. So it was always fun. My dad played in a band. He was like the guitarist in the band. Yeah, so it was good.... I liked to stay with my dad. So I would usually stay there and listen to him play in the band and listen to the adult sermon.... It was a nondenominational Christian church. It was really a nice place compared to the rest of my life, it really was a comfortable, nice place... a wonderful, beautiful, fun place.*

While this time with her dad was nice, things with her mom had only gotten worse. Her mother's new boyfriend was abusive, and domestic violence became the norm. For Nancy, life at home with mom was chaotic and often precarious. But at least she had her dad—her main source of love. He was the sober one. He was the steady, peaceful one. He was working to improve himself in all aspects of his life, from the financial to the spiritual. He was the one that she could call when things got too ugly at mom's.

And then, when Nancy was nine, he died.

> *One morning my grandma noticed he didn't get up to go to work. He had his own little business. He was a landscaper. She went in his bedroom and he was unconscious and gurgling blood. It ended up that he had an aneurysm, so he died like three weeks after that.*

With the death of her father, Nancy's already precarious world crumbled completely.

> *After my dad died, that was probably my worst life experience ever, like—the most painful. And there was nobody there to really—as a fourth grader, I was*

nine—so there was nobody in my life that was really stable enough to help me like deal with it in the ways you're supposed to help people deal with that kind of stuff. So my life, by fifth grade, things were just terrible. I was just an emotional wreck. Nobody knew what to do with me. I stopped doing homework. I would just have these breakdowns in the middle of the classroom, that kind of stuff. My mom was doing her own thing and not really helpful.... Life just really went downhill for me, and it would stay that way for a long time.

For most of her teenage years, Nancy's church attendance became sporadic. She moved from relationship to (sometimes abusive) relationship, she struggled to get by, she fought with her mother, and she got high a lot. She prayed now and then—asking God for help when needed. And her Christian faith got a serious dose of adrenaline in the wake of a powerful spiritual experience.

When I was 19 I was really, really heavily into drugs. And I was going out with this guy whose mom was now sober—like an ex-prostitute, heroin addict, whatever. And him and I used together. I just remember this one incident when she was at the house I was staying at and she prayed Satan out of me. We had this big crazy moment where she spoke in tongues and did the whole ritual and, like, I shook. I don't know, I remember that being a defining moment, like: "Yes, there is a God."... She was like casting the demons from the house.... She just started like praying the demons out of me.... I mean, I just remember it being so intense....I remember shaking and crying and falling to my knees.... I felt the realness of God and that God did love me.

Unfortunately, her sense of God's love didn't keep her from staying out of trouble. When she was 23, she got busted again and was sentenced to one year behind bars. Depressed and lonely, she turned to God again. She really needed the Lord this time, desperately. She cried out to Him to help her, to support her, to ease her pain. And it worked—she was comforted. She also started talking regularly with the prison chaplain about Christ. His words were also comforting. And she started reading the Bible a lot; it was, after all, the only book in prison that was consistently easy to obtain. She was also able to get a hold of the

Left Behind series, and although she couldn't quite come to terms with the whole business about the world's cataclysmic ending, she was moved by the powerful tale of the Christian forces of good prevailing over the Satanic forces of evil. It was like The Lord of the Rings—only true. At least she thought so at the time.

During this period of intense religiosity, she saw signs of God's mercy all around her:

> I remember one incident where there was a girl and she was in the jail cell next to me, and it turned out like we knew each other. And she was pregnant. And she was probably like 18 or 19—and they hadn't fed her. She was so hungry and I remember praying all night saying, "God, I'm not praying for myself, but I'm praying for Tina." So they brought her a sandwich, and I knew God was there.

When she got out of prison this time, she vowed never to return. She went straight to Alcoholics Anonymous, attended daily meetings, and she got sober—for good. After a year or so, her life had never been better. She was finally standing on her own two feet. She had a decent job. She started taking classes at her local community college. And then, after two or three years into this new and improved existence, she came to realize that she didn't believe in God anymore and that religion was (at best) not for her and (at worst) a bunch of baloney.

> I just kind of think that there is no God and there is no karma and there is no . . . I just have come to that place where . . . I don't know. I don't know what you call it, but it's just kind of where I'm at.

What happened? How did Nancy go from being so religious to being so secular? Before attempting to answer that, let's consider Rita's story. There are some differences in the journeys of these two women, but there are also some interesting similarities.

*   *   *

Rita's family was lower working-class. Her dad was a security guard, and her mom was a teacher's aide at an elementary school. They rented a small house down the street from a Lutheran church. Her folks were married in that church and Rita was baptized there, went to preschool there, was confirmed there, and went there every Sunday well into her teens.

Rita describes her mother as very devout:

> *My mom . . . had kind of a tough life growing up. Their life was really hard. She said that church was the first place she ever went where she was told that somebody would always love her, somebody would always . . . you know, she could always talk to, would never judge her. So it was something that was really important to her. . . . She definitely believed in an afterlife, she believed that God loves you and he would look after you.*

Rita's dad, however, was less markedly religious:

> *He goes to church, but I kind of feel he just does because of like tradition . . . like, he always went to church with my mom but—he never really talked about religion or what he believed. . . . You know, he would never make statements like "God has a plan" or anything like that.*

Growing up, Rita definitely took after her mother.

> *Yeah, I was totally believing. . . . I believed that there was God that could hear my prayers. . . . I believed that God cared about me, I believed that he was interested in my life and what was going on and that he would help me if I would pray to him or that he would help people that I loved if I prayed about that. I believed that God would judge me. Like, I felt like a really strong sense of conscience. . . . I mean, I would think really strongly about doing things, because I would think—not necessarily that it was good or bad—but that God wouldn't like it.*

Rita was active in her church youth group. At age 11, she tried reading the Bible all the way through. And she prayed regularly.

Things started to get rocky for Rita, however, once she hit her teenage years. She didn't get into as much trouble with the law as Nancy did, but she did party a lot—drinking and smoking pot. And she liked boys.

I lost my virginity before I was married, and that was something that I thought was like really important—that I was going to hold on to. And then I would still go to church, but like I would start crying—in church—like, uncontrollably. I would have panic attacks inside church because I felt like—I felt like it was almost a slap in God's face for me to even be there when I knew I was doing things that were wrong and I was still doing them. . . . Then one night I was so depressed and upset and I was like, "I don't even care, I'm going to smoke weed now." I probably smoked numerous joints. We smoked out of a pipe, we smoked out of a bong—for my first time. . . . Then came the drinking. I would sneak out of my house like every night and I would go hang out with boys, and the two boys that I smoked weed with for the first time, like I totally made out with them like in the same night at the same time. That was kind of . . . I mean it was really fun for me, but I felt like later. . . . I remember talking to my best friend about it and she quit being my friend. Like, she'd been my best friend since we were seven or eight and she basically told me that I was a slut even though I was just kissing. . . . I just felt really bad, like maybe I am making bad choices. Then I did coke, I did speed, and I did all kinds of other stuff. I had sex like numerous times with more people than I probably should have at that age. . . . I think that I started ditching school, I was—

And all the while you're going to church on Sundays?

Yeah. And I would start having fights with my mom because, you know, Saturday night all these things were happening and then Sunday I didn't want to get up early and go to church. A lot of times I felt sick or just tired because I'd just gotten home at six in the morning and then at eight, she's like, "Get up, you need to go to church." I'm like, "I don't want to go to church, I don't want to go." She would try to make me. She mostly did make me until like one day when—we'd gotten into a big fight and I'm like, "I'm not going, like I don't want to go—why should you have to make me go? Like, if you

want to go, that's fine." I know that I really hurt her feelings. I think she cried,
but I got to stay home that day and she never made me go again.

So when you're going through all this as a teenager, you're sort of
like, "I don't want to go to church anymore." But are you still
believing that there's a God...?

Oh, yeah, totally. Yeah, I totally did. I even, you know—I got married when I
was 19 and I was already pregnant at the time, and it was totally like—not a
shotgun wedding, but it was like, "Okay, we're pregnant, like, we should get
married." And I got married because I felt like that's what you should do. You
should have a family now—I messed up, I made a choice, I got pregnant, and
I ended up marrying a guy that was completely, like, a bad choice. A bad choice
to be a father, for one, and then a bad choice to be a husband too. But I felt like
I had to do it. I remember when I got married, like I cried and cried and cried
during the whole thing.

Did you feel like you had to get married because of parental expectations or because of God or...?

Oh, because of God. Definitely because of God.

Rita's life as a newlywed was difficult and depressing. A month
or so after giving birth to her first child, she was pregnant again,
and her husband was regularly unemployed and regularly
stoned. She was the only one consistently working, both inside
and outside of the home. Watching their debt grow, she found
herself looking for a second job—while her husband didn't even
have one. It quickly became apparent to her that this arrange-
ment wasn't going to work. Midway through her second pregnancy, she decided that she needed to change directions, and
fast. Despite the fact that she had only tried to do what she
thought would be best in the eyes of the Lord, she realized that
she had made a mistake marrying this man, and she knew that
she had to correct that mistake as soon as possible. She filed for
a divorce. They had been married for one year. Rita's husband

didn't have much interest in being with the children, and after the divorce he quickly vanished from their lives.

Now she found herself a single mom with two babies at the age of 20. No college education. No formal job training. No vocational skills. No financial support from mom and dad. But she did have one thing: self-motivation. She immediately set to work making the best of things, getting herself together, and improving life for herself and her kids. In addition to holding down two jobs, she applied for federal and county welfare assistance, which helped her make ends meet. The food stamps were the only thing keeping her and her kids from going hungry. And she started taking classes at her local community college, with an eye toward a better professional future.

> I realized that I was the only thing in my kids' life—that I had to straighten up, I had to get a good job, I had to get a good education, I had to do everything that I had to do for them.

During this period of clarified self-awareness and focused self-improvement, Rita didn't turn to God for comfort. She didn't pray for inspiration. She didn't turn to the church for help. In fact, she became an atheist.

* * *

Why did Nancy and Rita become secular?

One interesting factor to consider is when both of these women experienced their loss of faith. Both Rita and Nancy were at the points in their lives when they were improving themselves. Both had been religious children and teenagers—times when they weren't in control of their own lives or their own destinies. That is, they were both pious believers in God at times when they were young and/or dependent on others, when they were living relatively reckless lives, without much direction or guidance. But once they were somehow able to personally take control of their own lives as self-possessed, mature individuals, secularity ensued.

For both of them, it happened in their early twenties. Nancy had gotten sober (initially with the help of her belief in God, to be sure), and she was working in a secure job as an assistant to a man with a small business when her religiosity started to weaken. Rita was no longer partying hard or having casual sex, she was no longer living with an unemployed man that she didn't love, and her goal of being a good provider for her kids had become crystal clear. Soon after, she was an atheist. In short, both of these women lost their faith when they were feeling—perhaps for the first time—in control of their own destinies. The fact that Rita and Nancy both rejected religion at a period in their lives when they were working for the first time—making money and supporting themselves—suggests the possibility that there may be a connection at the broader, societal level to women's participation in the workforce and secularization. This is a theory posited by the British historian Callum Brown. In his fascinating book *The Death of Christian Britain* (2001), Brown reveals a strong correlation between the significant increase in British women joining the paid workforce in the 1960s and the subsequent decrease of religious belief and participation.

A second similarity is that for both Rita and Nancy, the move from religion to irreligion was sparked in part by a skeptical male acquaintance. In Nancy's case, it was her boss, Jason. He was a very nice, very kind man. He was successful and smart. He ran his own business, was a college graduate, and he seemed to know a lot about the world. On top of these impressive qualities, Nancy was deeply grateful that he had hired her, even though he knew full well that she was a recovering alcoholic and ex-con. He respected her, despite her past. He trusted her. And she in turn respected and trusted him. Then one day at work, he brought up the fact that he was a nonbeliever.

> I was probably over a year sober and I was working at a place called Pools and Spas. My boss there . . . he was just, like, one day: "There's no God." I was kind of like—I didn't really say anything. I was just, like: what is he talking about?! I think that was the first time I had heard anybody say there's no God. I was

just kind of taken aback. He was like, "Look at the pain and suffering that goes on in the world, blah, blah, this, that, and the other." I thought about it more and more. I just remember thinking—in a way—how dare you? I mean, he knew a little bit about me. He knew that I was in the program [Alcoholics Anonymous]. He knew some of my struggles to some degree....I feel like I remember being kind of pissed off, like, how could he know that? And then at the same time, like, the other part of my brain kind of said: well, it's not completely absurd....I started questioning God when I started working for Jason...thinking maybe there's no God.

Rita had a similar experience. The man who initially opened up Rita's thinking was her first postdivorce boyfriend, Stuart. They had been dating for a couple of months, and he started spending the night at her place more and more frequently (although they weren't having sex at this point, Rita is quick to add). One night, after the kids were asleep, they were laying on the couch talking when Rita asked him about his faith. His response took her by surprise:

I remember asking him: do you believe in God? And he was like, "I don't know, I don't think so, really." I remember getting really upset... but he was the first person that I had ever talked to that had even been—and he kind of framed it—I don't know...I was like—oh my God. It was a shock to me that this could happen. He was somebody that I thought was really, really smart. He was a good person; he came from a pretty normal family. I mean, like, he...was a pretty, you know, okay guy. I just remember thinking like, "Wow, like if it's possible to doubt and..." It kind of opened the door....I would say that that was THE turning point where I was—where it's possible to doubt it.

If these conversations were the first cracks in their faith, higher education widened those cracks. Nancy and Rita started taking classes at their local community colleges. These classes definitely had a corrosive effect on their religiosity. Or, rather, as they would put it, an enlightening effect.

Rita recalled:

I took a world religions class. I was just really fascinated by, like, the different kinds of beliefs that people had and I kind of really liked Hinduism for a while—because the religion teacher that I had was, you know, "Hinduism accepts everybody." So I thought that was really cool...and then I started to kind of branch out into, like, you know, looking at Buddhism or Taoism or Hinduism or whatever and just kind of seeing there's different ways of looking at things...and then I think that it really started snowballing.

For Rita—and many others—learning about other religions threatened her deeply held faith because it made apparent the unavoidable: there are many other religions out there, all with their deep traditions and theological creeds. And the adherents of these other religions generally think that theirs is the correct, best, or ultimately true one. And who can say who is right? Furthermore, there were elements of other religions that Rita found attractive or commendable, things absent from Christianity. This recognition caused her to be more open-minded about other possible ways of believing—or not believing at all.

Nancy's immersion into community college was also significant. The classes she took in psychology, sociology, and history made her familiar with new theories about what it means to be human and how and why people do what they do, think what they think, and believe what they believe. These classes caused Nancy to come face to face with the unavoidable insight that our beliefs are largely culturally determined, that our religion is often a result of social-ization, and that our specific religious identity is usually the result of random historical circumstances beyond our control. She also became familiar with some of the psychological underpinnings of religious faith, and the result was that she became more self-re-flective. When one learns about the ways in which religion can be socially constructed, the result can sometimes be a decreased surety in the grand cosmic truth claims of one's own religion. The things Nancy learned in her classes were clearly mind-expanding, and they quickly chipped away at her Christianity.

These were the main similarities in Rita's and Nancy's apos-tasies: both lost their faith at the point in life when they were successfully in control of their own destinies for the first time, both were introduced to skeptical ideas by men in their lives that they liked and respected, and both found their immersion into community college an eye-opening experience that challenged their deeply held religious beliefs.

But there were also some factors that were unique to each woman. Looking back on her life now, Nancy considers the premature death of her father as a key initial factor in her eventual embrace of atheism:

> *I'd probably start with my dad dying. And I'd probably say if God wanted to take care of me, if God wanted me to have a great life that involved maybe college after high school instead of drugs, then he would have took my mom—honestly. I mean, my dad could have taken way better care of us than my mom did.... There was a lot of abuse—verbal, physical, sexual, all these things. I mean...you can't tell me that it was because of somebody's "free will" that I got my ass beat every day. That doesn't make sense...as an adult reflecting on my childhood, I would say—no, it doesn't make sense and I don't believe.*

I reminded Nancy that when times were rough she did turn to God. Maybe things were good now for her, so she can sort of say she doesn't believe. But what if tomorrow she were to get cancer or her boyfriend gets hit by a car or she started using again— would she find Jesus again?

> *I would say I wouldn't. This feeling that I have now is much more compelling. See—I don't know. I feel like now it's more compelling than that ever was. Like it makes sense.*

As for Rita, her life continued to improve after she attended community college (and stopped being a Christian). She earned a scholarship to transfer to a private, liberal arts college. Once there, she excelled, got straight A's, and graduated with honors. She and her boyfriend recently bought a home, and her children are doing well in school. Rita believes that these successes came from her own hard work, self-reliance, and "being really smart." And she is convinced that being secular gave her confidence and clear vision through it all.[4]

*   *   *

Any one of the specific factors that Rita and Nancy identified, singled out on its own, might not explain much. Take the matter of going to community college: most people who go to community college—even those who take world religions classes and loads of social science—don't become apostates. They leave community college just as religious as when they began. Or take the matter of having male acquaintances who are nonbelievers; surely most women who have had a nonbelieving boyfriend or a nonbelieving boss do not go on to become atheists themselves. It's the same for losing a parent in childhood: most people who experience such a loss maintain their faith throughout their lives. Even the fact that both of these women became irreligious at times in their lives when they were becoming successfully independent may just be coincidental. However, if we take all of the above-discussed factors together, perhaps we approach an answer in explaining how and why these two women—two very unlikely candidates for atheism—rejected their religion.

There's one final aspect of these women's apostasies that strikes me as noteworthy, and that has to do with the matter of morality. Both women could easily be classified as "more moral" as atheists than when they were religious. In the seven or eight years since Nancy lost her faith, she has not been arrested, and for good reason: she hasn't broken any laws. Nor has she gotten drunk or high. She hasn't been living in a way that one would classify as reckless, self-destructive, or unethical. It is quite the opposite; she has slowly but steadily continued on with her education while working as a waitress, and as of this writing, she is one year away from obtaining her bachelor's degree. And she describes her relationship with her long-time boyfriend as healthy and happy, with plans in the works for a wedding. Things weren't always this good or stable for Nancy, and as we saw above, it was actually when she was religious that she was breaking the law, doing drugs, and living with abusive boyfriends. Clearly, belief in God didn't curb her unhealthy behavior. The unavoidable truth is that while Nancy was religious, it was still quite easy for her to act irresponsibly and immorally. Yet since she has lost her faith, acting responsibly morally has been quite natural and easy. I asked her about this:

> I'm still a good person even though I can say I don't believe in God and I know I'm still a good person...yeah, I meet good people every day who don't go to church and don't pray and I don't necessarily know if they do or don't believe in God. I meet a lot of really terrible people and I read a lot of terrible things about people who know there is nothing else but God...so, I mean...I know that I'm a good moral person, and I used to think that in order to be that I had to...God was a part of that, but I realize that it's not.

Why are you a moral person then if you don't think God's watching you anymore?

> Because that's just what I think everybody should do. I mean there's really no...I mean—not that I haven't done bad things, but I don't know. It just seems like the world goes a little smoother when people are nice to each other. It just feels better, even though there's no ultimate reward for me at the end of my day, in my head it feels better.

In the few years since Rita lost her faith, she has also lived a moral, ethical life. She stopped the excessive partying and drinking. Having recently graduated from college, she got a secure job as an assistant director of a nonprofit organization that works on combating social problems plaguing poor communities. For the first time in many years, she has health insurance. She works hard, and she helps out at her children's school when possible. While she believed strongly in Jesus, God, heaven, and hell, she still did things that many would consider sinful. Yet as her faith evaporated, so too did most of her sinning.

Interviewing individuals like Rita and Nancy made me wonder what postreligious life is like for other apostates. How do they see the world? Are they more moral now, or has their morality slipped since losing faith in God? Do they fear death? What is the meaning of life? Do they miss anything about being religious?

8

✧

The Apostate Worldview

It is, without a doubt, one of the most common of notions: morality comes from belief in God. This idea that secularity is somehow linked to moral depravity is truly widespread. For example, in his best-selling book, *The Purpose Driven Life*, Evangelical pastor Rick Warren argues that people who don't hold biblically based religious beliefs have no motivation to be good or ethical; rather, they would lead lives of selfish indulgence and cold indifference to others.[1]

There is one key problem, however, with this millennia-old thesis: it is demonstrably false. "The claim that atheists are somehow likely to be immoral or dishonest," observes psychologist Benjamin Beit-Hallahmi, "has long been disproven by systematic studies."[2] Indeed, a plethora of sociological, psychological, and criminological studies over many decades has shown that secular people are just as decent and moral as religious people, and they may actually be even *more* decent and moral, at least on certain measures.[3] As gerontologist Vern Bengston found in his research comparing religious and secular families, "Most of the non-religious were quite articulate about [their] ethics and value systems. Many were more passionate and articulate about their ethical precepts than some of the 'religious' individuals in our study."[4] And it is important to note that atheists are notably underrepresented in America's prisons.[5] And the least religious countries in the world today tend to have the lowest violent crime and murder rates.[6] This holds true within the United States as well, where murder and violent crime rates are markedly higher in the Bible Belt than in the less religious regions of the country.[7] On top of all of this, studies have shown that nonreligious people tend to be less supportive of the death penalty as well as the governmental use of torture than their religious peers.[8]

Apostates have lived on both sides of the fence: they've been religious, and they've been secular. How did their morality change as a result? In the aftermath of their loss of faith, do they subsequently experience a loss of moral direction? Do they find it harder to make ethical choices and live moral lives? The answer to both of these questions appears to be an unequivocal "no." They did not experience a loss of moral focus after rejecting religion and they did not find it harder to make moral choices once they had abandoned their faith. This finding helps to establish the important fact that morality is certainly possible without religion or a belief in God. But I would even take it a step farther and argue that morality actually *improves* after individuals undergo a transition from being religious to secular. As many apostates emphatically explained to me, their own personal morality was sharpened, enhanced, and ultimately became more mature once they left religion behind.

MORALITY AFTER RELIGION

Many apostates said that while they were religious, their concept of what it meant to be moral tended to focus on specific, "taboo" things, such as not masturbating, not having premarital sex, or not doing drugs. If you resisted such temptations, you were "moral." Morality essentially tended to be a sort of laundry list of do's and don'ts: do pray, do read the Bible, don't drink alcohol, don't look at pornography. Stealing was also considered bad, as was lying—especially to one's parents. Now, as apostates, there is less concern with these specific do's and don'ts, especially as related to sexual matters, drinking, or other such private indulgences. What is important to apostates is how they treat other people. Stealing and lying are of course still considered immoral, but the basic underlying reasons as to *why* these acts are seen as immoral has changed. As religious believers, they felt it was wrong to steal or lie because it was bad in the eyes of God. As secular nonbelievers, they see stealing and lying as wrong because it causes others pain or loss, and it helps foster a world lacking in trust or concern for the well-being of others. While religious, they felt bad about lying primarily because they knew it would upset God, and they feared his condemnation. As apostates, they feel bad about lying because they know they have wronged someone, and they understand that lying ultimately has negative social and emotional consequences. Thus, the most important, fundamental element of apostate morality is its underlying motivation. While religious, most men and women I interviewed were motivated to be moral largely out of a sense of fear: fear of hell, fear of God's anger, fear of a priest's pious rebukes. Being moral was also enmeshed with obedience: obedience to God's will, obedience to the Bible, or obedience to the pastor's word. However, as apostates, fear and obedience are no longer the principal motivational mechanisms underlying morality. Rather, apostate morality is based upon understanding the ramifications of one's actions, having genuine empathy for others, and realizing that the world is simply a better place when people act ethically toward one another. In fact, if we consider the common model of moral development as articulated by social psychologist Lawrence Kohlberg, it is clear that secular morality is more advanced and more mature, existing at a higher stage of ethical development than religious morality.[9]

Chuck, age 36, is a former Pentecostal Christian. He feels that he is more moral now as an atheist than he ever was as a believer. For him, obedience to God out of fear of eternal damnation does not render an individual moral:

If someone takes a gun to my head and tells me to go to the ATM and with-
draw the maximum amount and give it to me—and I do so because I don't

want to be shot in the head—I don't call myself generous. So, I don't think that you can call yourself "good" for obeying God. That doesn't—to me— that's not good. That's not goodness. . . . One thing that drives me nuts is when religious people claim all the time that "you cannot know good unless you know God." I think it's exactly the opposite: you cannot possibly be good if you're just being good because you don't want to suffer eternal punishment.

Stanley is 38 years old, and he grew up in a small town in Texas. He was deeply religious and had been groomed from an early age for the pulpit. But as he got older, and walked away from Christianity, his morality became much more secular:

I think that there's a lot of benefits from truthfulness, from trying not to harm other people or other things, and to try and minimize your negative impact on the world. You don't have to have religion for that, I don't think. I mean, there are tons of reasons for that that make much more sense to me than worrying about if I'm going to be punished if I do or don't do this kind of stuff.

From Henry, age 41, and a former Baptist:

If I screw someone over, the immediate consequence is I feel awful and when you live with yourself and you feel awful about yourself, there's no escaping it. It's a horrible thing . . . mainly, it's my own conscience. I just don't want to be the cause of suffering for others. I think that morality comes from simply being human. Having the senses to perceive pain and suffering. . . . It doesn't take a religion to understand that we're social primates that have to get along, and we're trying to do that. When I was a Christian, I remember being moti- vated by what I thought God wanted . . . now, I feel like I am good because I've made the decision to be good.

Milton, age 45 and a former devout Catholic who is now an athe- ist, puts it this way:

I think societies work better when people are deciding for themselves how they should act towards each other and . . . not factoring their ethical decisions through this third party. They're not outsourcing their moral decisions. They're making them themselves.

In *Mere Christianity*, C. S. Lewis argues that human beings cannot be truly good or moral without faith in God and without submission to the will of Christ. Unfortunately, Lewis does not provide any actual data for his assertions. They are nothing more than the mild musings of a wealthy British man, pondering the state of humanity's soul between his sips of tea. Had Lewis actually familiarized himself with real human beings of the secular sort, perhaps sat and talked with them, he would have had to reconsider this notion. As so many apostates explained to me, morality is most certainly possible beyond the confines of faith. Can people be good without God? Can a moral orientation be sustained and developed outside of a religious context? The answer to both of these questions is a resounding yes.[10]

THE MEANING OF LIFE

Another widespread assumption is that religion maintains a unique, privileged position as something that infuses life with meaning. And just like the age-old assertion that people need religion in order to have morals, it is often argued that people need religion in order to experience a deep, satisfying, meaningful life. I've heard it many times: without religion or belief in the existence of God, life is somehow empty, vacuous, anemic, purposeless. Again, C. S. Lewis provides us with a good example. Throughout the latter half of *Mere Christianity*, Lewis argues that life is empty without an abiding faith in Jesus Christ—it becomes a charade of selfishness, sexual immorality, and darkness. Indeed, a life without Christ is, at root, "only hatred, loneliness, despair, rage, ruin, and decay."[11] No equivocation there.

But if we simply look at the worldviews of the apostates I interviewed, we can see that Lewis was way off the mark. Most of them see no ultimate, grand, or magically divine meaning of life, but they don't despair. Rather, they believe that each person must find his or her own meaning—which, for apostates, seems to be easy enough.[12]

Consider Joanna, age 24, a former Catholic who now describes herself as agnostic:

> To me, what brings meaning to life is making the world as much of my own heaven as I can.... We don't have any proof of what happens after we die. Why wouldn't we live this life to the most full and honest potential that we can?

According to Daphne, age 29 and a former Evangelical Protestant who now describes herself as secular:

> I think the meaning of life is just relationships with people. I don't need to have God love me because I have friends and family that love me and I think it's about being the best person that I can be and the best friend that I can be and having relationships here with real people.

Scott is 36 years old, and he was born and raised in North Dakota among conservative Lutherans. Today, he's agnostic. Here is his take on the meaning of life:

> The meaning of life is to find your purpose.... I think the purpose is sort of a hybrid of trying to advance you and your family and do something good, but more importantly, to leave something good behind for the rest of humankind.

Eugene is 72 years old. Born in Atlanta, he was raised a Protestant, but he came to realize that he was an atheist when he was in his twenties. When I asked Eugene what he thought was the meaning of life, he replied,

> I don't know if there's a meaning to life.... I guess I'd have to say as far as the meaning of life, who knows? You know, generally compassion, fairness...those kinds of things. So if you ask me what's the meaning of life, I have a hard time

answering that because I don't know if there is a meaning in life. I suppose the purpose of life . . . is to try to have as good a life as you can, be kind and good to other people, try to do something useful with your life. . . . I don't look for the meaning of life somewhere up there. Here we are on earth, let's do the best we can to live in harmony, live a good life, try to be happy as you can.

Although Eugene doesn't believe in a grand or God-inspired meaning of life, he is in no sense an apathetic nihilist. He's lived his life as a committed family man. He taught high school biology for 30 years. He loves to hike. He reads a lot and has strong opinions about politics. Eugene, and others like him whom I interviewed, are living proof that it is clearly possible to live a meaningful life beyond the confines of religion. For most, life after or without religion does not result in anomie, depression, or a paralyzing sense of meaningless.

Consider Henry, a 41-year-old former Catholic, who ventured more into Protestant circles in his teens, only to become an atheist in his early twenties. As he explained:

To me, life has meaning simply because we're here, whether we like it or not. And there are many ways we can improve our situation and help others who are in need. . . . In essence, I believe life is its own reward. . . . After divesting myself of religion, life in general finally made sense. I found life MORE enjoyable. . . . Not believing in some afterlife or "second coming" means I am more focused on the here and now, preserving life, preventing suffering, doing my part to be environmentally conscious. I no longer see this body and Earth as some lobby for an afterlife. This life is precious.

DEATH

In 2005, I moved to Denmark with my family for over a year, to study what life is like in one of the least religious countries in the world. Over the course of that year, I conducted in-depth interviews with nearly 150 people, asking them about their religious beliefs (or lack thereof), views about life and death, and much more. One of the most consistent findings from that research concerned death. Among these contemporary Scandinavians, what I found was a widely shared, remarkably common orientation to death that could be characterized as one of simple, stoic acceptance. The majority of those I interviewed said that they didn't worry or obsess too much about death, but they calmly understood that it was the natural, inevitable conclusion to every life. And there's nothing afterwards—no heaven, no hell. For most Scandinavians, this is the only life we will ever have. And that's okay. Even good. Or if not good, well, then just the way it is.[13]

I was curious if American apostates would have a similar view of death. So I asked them: what do they think happens after we die? What are your feelings about your own imminent demise?

Chuck, age 36 and a former Pentecostal Christian, offered a response that was fairly typical among most of those interviewed:

> I think that it's likely that we die and we just die and we carry on through our progeny and through the good works that we've done and the bad works that we've done and so forth. I believe in karma—in the sense that it's a force that carries on sort of like a ripple effect through the universe. So, I don't know that I really believe in an afterlife existence. Actually—I don't believe in an afterlife existence. But I remain open.

How does it make you feel—not knowing—or thinking there isn't an afterlife existence?

> It makes me feel just fine. I really think that mortality is the savior of humankind. For me, it's a good thing because it means that what we do right now is super important because you only get one chance to do it and, you know, you never know when your time is going to be up....I guess for me it's not a bad thing at all. It's a redemptive thing.

From Penny, age 29, another common response:

> I don't really think anything happens. I think we die and it's over.

Isn't that a terrifying thought?

I think it was originally. But I don't think it is anymore. I think it makes the life that we have more valuable and more important. It makes me want to have more of an influence on the world while I'm here because this is it. This is my only shot.

Most apostates shared similar sentiments. Clearly, Scandinavia isn't the only place on earth where one can quite easily find men and women, of all ages, who peacefully accept the unavoidable fact of their own eventual demise, who either don't believe in life after death or simply aren't too sure about there being any real postmortality possibilities—and they are okay with that. This lack of belief in life after death, or a lack of surety that there is any more after this earthly existence, does not unhinge these apostates. It does not shatter their knees or destroy their wills. They carry on with their lives, finding fulfillment. Clearly, life can be enjoyed while maintaining the belief or suspicion that this is all there is. In fact, for some people, believing that "this is all there is" makes life better, richer, and more precious.

LOSS

Is there a downside to rejecting one's religion? The answer, at least for some, is that apostasy certainly has its costs. First off, the rejection of religion can sometimes render one an outcast, straining and even destroying personal relationships with family and friends. But there is more. Some people, such as Nathan, miss the powerful feeling of being connected to God that had been such a major part of their lives for many years.

The absolute best thing about being religious—or I should say, being an Evangelical Christian—was the deep personal relationship that I thought I had with God. I mean, it's a powerful thing to imagine that the God of the universe is on your side, talking to you on a daily basis, and that you're actually communicating with that God. That's powerful. And I think that gave me some confidence, and it gave me a sense of—that my future was really sealed and that God had good things waiting for me—a sense of optimism. . . . Not only that—the worship experience. To this day, I'm trying to figure out how— when you have really powerful praise and worship when you're with a group of people—that's a powerful experience. I do miss that—something that gives me the same kind of sense of passion.

For Trent, age 19, leaving the church and rejecting Christianity was, at least in the first year or two, quite hard:

It was a little bit saddening for me because I had used it as like a way to feel more secure in life, and felt like I had a purpose and a direction. Losing that made me really feel, like, lost. Like, well, if I'm not so sure that there is this Christian God or if like the Bible like is the word of God, then like what am I doing here? What am I supposed to be? And . . . I still don't necessarily have a clear sense of purpose for my life. Which is something that I miss. Because it just feels so much more secure, like: "I KNOW why I'm here . . . I KNOW my goals." Like, I don't really have that anymore. But . . . it's not as bad as it was at first . . . I've moved on a bit.

For Tony, age 47, his loss of faith was not something he "chose," but it was something that just happened over time. And while Tony certainly prefers his irreligious worldview to his former Christian worldview, he can still recall the personal and psychological benefits of his former belief system:

There's a sense of purpose, there's a sense of assurance—assurance not on every doctrinal point, but an assurance of who Christ is, the centrality of that—a direction. I was fairly focused that way. It gave you somewhere to work towards. I think that was some of the value there. . . . The worst thing [about being a nonbeliever] . . . is there's not a firm—it's mushy. And mushy's both good and bad. But it's mushy, and it's sand and it moves and it changes and it's hard to reconcile things at times. It's hard to understand—you go one way and a few months later you think, "Oh, I don't know if I believe that."

You're going back and forth and back and forth on things. . . . I also do miss a
sense of community and direction.

Tony was not the only apostate to mention a loss of community.
In fact, it was the most common answer expressed when it came
to the downside of apostasy, coming up in interview after interview. And the fact that so many apostates cited the loss of
community as the worst thing about their loss of faith tells us a
lot about that most important and powerful function of religion
in many people's lives—it provides meaningful social interaction. As Mark Regnerus notes, "The local religious congregation
is the most popular voluntary organization in America and often
provides adherents with readily available social networks."[14]
Religion is, above all things, a steady and solid source of communal bonding. Angels, demons, prophets, miracles, saviors, sac-
rifices, prayers, songs, sacred writings, moral teachings, and
promises of eternal life notwithstanding, a major reason for why
people are religiously involved is because it provides them with
community, a sense of belonging, a social system, a consistent
and steady home away from home where people care for one
another, know one another, support one another, inquire about
each other's kids, make arrangements for each other's funerals,
celebrate each other's joys, and live together year after year in a
seasonal cycle of meaningful human interaction and communal
purpose. As Greg Epstein acknowledges, for many people, religion "is about group identification—the community and the connections we need to live."[15] The theme song from the top 1980s
TV show *Cheers* says it best: we all want to go somewhere where
everybody knows our name and is always glad we came—a place
where everybody's troubles are all the same. And if this place also
channels people's energies into doing good deeds and feeling a
sense of higher purpose and intimacy with a supposed divine
being, all the better. The secular life is largely absent of such a
place, and apostates often feel that absence.

Max, age 65, has been nonreligious since he was 14 years old.
And he has always felt that the one thing religious people have

that secular people lack is a strong community. He remembers how important church life was to his family, particularly his own father, who turned to his congregation for comfort when his wife died:

> I think there was a lot of comfort in our case. And I feel this is a very powerful force in religion, and one that nonreligious people haven't found how to deal with yet, and that's the congregation and the camaraderie between those who believe....
>
> That was very strong in our case. My dad went to many of the church-related things and we had several friends within the church that we often ate at their house or they ate at ours. We would call on them for help in a situation, and they were very helpful, like when my mother died. They brought food. That is a strength of religion that we're lacking.

Carol, age 21, said,

> I miss the community—the best thing about being religious is the community. I had a very different connection with my church friends than I had with my school friends. We were just...I mean, we were in the good fight together. We were just involved in so many different activities.

Human beings are social animals, and without social interaction, we get depressed. Indeed, the very first major study in the development of the discipline of sociology, published toward the end of the 1800s, was Emile Durkheim's *Suicide*, and the key finding in that groundbreaking study was that suicide rates are higher where there is less social integration and people are relatively isolated from one another, while conversely, suicide rates are lower where social life is dense and enmeshed, and people are well-integrated with one another. Fast-forward about 100 years to another major sociological study—Robert Putnam's best-selling *Bowling Alone*—and we are presented with similar findings. Putnam found that social pathologies are worse in societies marked by low levels of social integration and "social capital," whereas societies in which people are socially engaged and communally involved are characterized by numerous indicators of well-being, prosperity, and social harmony. I have no doubt that the numerous studies showing the degree to which religious people tend to experience better or higher levels of well-being than nonreligious people can be attributed to the social, communal aspect of religious involvement.[16] People who belong to religious congregations will generally feel better and even be healthier than people who don't—simply because being part of a united, hope-driven, communal group is a sustaining, positive experience for most people, while isolation often isn't.

LIBERATION

Every single apostate agreed that the rewards of a more secular orientation far outweigh the costs. While there was much to be lost in rejecting their faith, there was far more to be gained. When I asked how it felt to lose their religious beliefs and/or leave their religion—and what the best thing about being an apostate was—my interviewees had quite a lot to say. This was often one of the high points of each interview, when I could sense people's demeanors brighten a bit as they spoke of the joys of apostasy. For these men and women, being nonreligious was liberatory. It meant being more open to others and the possibilities of the world, being more truthful with oneself about one's inner convictions, being free.[17]

Daphne, age 38, and a former Christian, described her apostasy this way:

> It's very liberating to feel like I'm in charge of my life. And I don't have to buy into these things and I can think for myself and can figure things out on my own and can still be a good person. And I don't have to be so judgmental about other people because they don't believe the same thing. You can appreciate other people in a different way and not feel sorry for them. Because that was a big thing—you kind of feel sorry for non-Christians because they just don't get it and, you know, you can witness to them, but then if they don't accept—they're going to hell. It's just a weird way of looking at the world. It's like "us"

and "them" which—it doesn't have to be us and them. Which it's not any-
more, which is nice.

Judy, age 27, is a former religious Jew:

The best thing—I feel like I see things pretty clearly for myself. I feel like I'm
governing my own path.... I see the world in the way that I want to see the
world and not in the way that books are telling me to see the world. I'm able
to sort of draw from lots of different perspectives and kind of—experiences—
and kind of glean my own understanding and I like that.

From David, age 58, and a former Jehovah's Witness:

I feel very liberated... very, very liberated and enlightened. I feel very free.
The freedom that I enjoy, it's... it's refreshing, to say the least.... Now I am
free from the fear of religion and the clutches... I don't have anybody
controlling what I have to think, what I have to read, what I have to say, who
to marry, how to make love... none of that. I am free to do what I need to do
or what I have to do within the concepts of civil laws.

From Haneefa, age 26, and a former Muslim:

I must tell you when I let go of religion, one thing I felt was relief. I feel a
profound sense of relief. I don't have any more unanswered questions. I
know there's science to explain it and everything makes sense to me now. I
can just live my life knowing I have control of my life. There is no afterlife.
This is it, make the most of it, and that's why I feel a great sense of relief.

*   *   *

In America today, there is a stigma attached to being openly godless.[18] Atheists and nonreligious people are not well liked. For
instance, a 2006 study found that atheists are perhaps the most
despised group within the United States. When people were
asked which of the following groups "shares my vision of
American society," out of a list that included Muslims, homosex-

uals, Jews, Hispanics, African Americans, immigrants, and so on, atheists came in last place. And in a subsequent question about whether one would disapprove if one's child married someone from a list of minority groups (Muslims, Jews, Hispanics, African Americans, etc.), again atheists fared the worst, with nearly half of Americans stating that they would disapprove of their child marrying an atheist. The authors of this study concluded that "atheists are at the top of the list of groups that Americans find problematic."[19] And a 2002 Pew Forum on Religion and Public Life survey found that 54% of Americans have a mostly or very unfavorable opinion of atheists (the most disliked group of all options presented), and just over 28% have a mostly or very unfavorable opinion of "people who are not religious."[20] Furthermore, a 1999 Gallup Poll found that when people were asked if they would feel comfortable voting for president someone who was a woman, or Jewish, Catholic, Mormon, Black, a homosexual, atheist, and so on, atheists again came in last; while over 90% of Americans said they would feel comfortable voting for a woman, Black, Jew, or Catholic candidate, and over 70% for a Mormon, and nearly 60% for a homosexual, only 49% said they would feel comfortable voting for an atheist for president.[21]

But it isn't just within public opinion polls that one finds a decidedly negative appraisal of secular people. John Dominic Crossan has equated atheism with "the state of being a sociopath or a psychopath."[22] John D. Caputo has written that people who don't love God aren't "worth a tinker's damn" and that anyone who isn't theistically religious is nothing more than a "selfish and pusillanimous curmudgeon... a loveless lout."[23] Rodney Stark, a sociologist of religion, has publicly described nonbelieving, irreligious people as "prickly" and "just angry."[24] And, of course, according to the pastor Rick Warren, people who don't believe in, worship, and obediently obey God are directionless, self-absorbed humans whose life has no purpose.

Sociopathic, angry, loveless, purposeless—are these the proper adjectives to accurately describe apostates, most of whom are atheists or agnostics? No. Not even close. No one who sits down with former believers and talks to them in depth about their lives, values, experiences, and personal worldviews could ever offer up such a flagrantly mistaken appraisal. Men and women who have rejected their religion in favor of a more secular worldview do not live without purpose or love, and they are not immoral curmudgeons, living heartless and empty lives predicated on self-indulgence and immorality. The vast majority of apostates I met live goal-filled lives characterized by direction and achievement. Most have graduated from college, and many possess advanced degrees. They have good jobs. The majority enjoy meaningful relationships with spouses, children, parents, lovers, relatives, friends, and colleagues. They find sustaining purpose and joy in their secular lives, and they believe that the lack of an afterlife actually heightens the purpose and meaning of this life. They accept the finality of their own deaths, and the knowledge of their own mortality does not render them detached or depressed but actually serves to increase their love of life. As for morality, most apostates find that their sense of right and wrong—their ethical compass—has improved and strengthened in the wake of their apostasy. And while they may experience a certain degree of loss as a result of their rejection of religion—particularly in terms of communal ties—what they have gained from their loss of faith is a sense of freedom, liberation, openness, and truthfulness.

But aren't apostates angry? Sure, at certain times during various interviews, anger would surface. There was Jack, who still harbors some resentment toward the priests in his Catholic high school who used to yell at him and regularly "beat the hell" out of him in the locker room. There was Rachel, who still feels a sting of anger when she recalls how her Jehovah's Witness parents refused to allow her younger brother to receive a desperately needed blood transfusion as he lay dying on a cold hospital bed. There was Victor, who finds it annoying when the coaches of his son's baseball team require that all the boys form a group huddle and pray, with eyes closed and hats off, before each game. There was also Guillermo, who became irate when talking about how several of his cousins were molested by a Catholic priest back in the 1980s. There were many other apostates who expressed anger toward clergy that they felt were hypocritical; toward religious teachings that they felt had been detrimental to their personal growth and well-being; toward parents and grandparents who had instilled such a dreaded fear of hell into their young imaginations; toward fellow congregants who expressed such hostility toward gay rights, vegetarianism, women's rights, or human rights; and toward relatives who condemned them as worthless, evil, or immoral for having rejected religion. But is anger their general or overriding disposition? Absolutely not. Anger was merely one emotion that had a tendency to bubble up at punctuated moments during interviews, when specific memories or topics came forth, prodded by my specific questions. By and large, the vast majority of apostates that I interviewed were kind, open, friendly, thoughtful, content, and optimistic, and they even expressed respect for certain aspects of religion and acceptance of people who are still religious. A fine example is Eugene. Although he realized that he was an atheist when he was in his twenties, he married a Catholic woman and had no problem raising his children with her in that tradition.

> I don't feel any animosity about religion....Actually, when I develop friendships, it doesn't seem to matter....I have friends now I know are quite religious, but we just don't get into it. We don't discuss it. It's just—to me—it's irrelevant to the friendship, or to even being a good human being, whether you are or not. I take the view that if your religion helps you and you feel good about it and you feel comfortable and you feel this is the core of your being, then by all means you should continue with that...as long as you're comfortable with it.

The notion that apostates are riddled with hostility, the claim that secular people are nothing buy angry curmudgeons, the insistence that one needs religion or faith in God to be moral, the belief that all humans fear death and that without a belief in immortality life would be unbearable, and the idea that without religion life is somehow meaningless—all of these widely touted assertions are simply untrue. There is no empirical data supporting their validity, and in fact there is a growing body of evidence that flatly contradicts them as nothing more than unsubstantiated stereotypes.

9

༺✻༻

All in the Family?

While many people I interviewed described both of their parents as being religious, others painted a different picture. Often, apostates had at least one parent who was somewhat nonreligious. I say "somewhat" nonreligious, because the depth of their distance from or disinterest in religion varied. Some were outright atheists, proud and outspoken in their secularity. But others were simply unenthusiastic about religion, humbly indifferent, but went along with it anyway, just because their husband or wife wanted them to.

For example, Mercedes described her family this way:

I grew up in a very traditional Catholic family—and more on the side of my mom. My Dad not so much. My Dad basically didn't really have a religion.... My Dad really didn't care. He never opposed my mom and he allowed us to go through baptism, confirmation, church, and he was always present at those religious events. But he—he never had a religion. But he obeyed the rules of the family, which was basically to do what my mom said [laughter].... My mom always prayed—and she's still praying—for his conversion, you know [laughter].

Haneefa had a similar upbringing:

It was mostly my mom who would tell me these [Islamic] stories. My dad almost never talked about it. So my mom, like, right before going to bed, she would tell me stories and I remember asking her, you know, "What's heaven like?" Things like that, when I was a kid. When I got to high school, she did hire a mullah to teach my brother and I how to read the Qu'ran. . . . Dad just never, ever talked about it at all. So I think he just let my mom handle the religious stuff.

For Sasha, her dad was the religious one:

My mother—she would go with us [to synagogue], but I think it was mostly because—just—my sister and I were younger so she just wanted to come with us and make sure we didn't fidget and everything [laughter]. But I don't really know how much she bought into Judaism. I think she did it for my Dad. She knew that it was really important to my Dad and his family . . . but eventually, she stopped going, so like, it would just be me and my Dad going.

Chuck's father felt more strongly:

My dad was absolutely atheist. Not agnostic—he was an atheist. He was into reading philosophy, he was like . . . my dad—hated church, hated it . . . as a matter of fact, what would happen . . . is that we would go to church on Sundays with my mom and then we would come home and my dad would be working in the garage. My dad was into rock collecting. He had a rock tumbler and all kinds of stuff. So he would be working in the garage and my brother and I would go out into the garage and my dad would counteract what we just learned [laughter] by reading to us or talking about philosophies or whatever.

Person after person, in interview after interview, would recall or recount how at least one of their parents—usually the father— was not all that religious. Approximately half of those I interviewed had at least one parent who was somewhat, if not decidedly, irreligious. Clearly, parental influence is a significant ingredient in apostasy. In fact, according to Hart Nelson, in American families back in the 1980s, where the father had no religion but the mother did, about one-sixth of the children grew up to become nonreligious. If the mother had no religion but the father did, then about half of their children grew up to be nonreligious; if both parents were irreligious, about 85% of such children grew up to be secular themselves.[1] And this should come as no surprise; decades of research have verified the undeniable fact that parental influence is one of—if not *the*—most important determinants of religious identity. It appears to be a significant determinant of irreligious identity as well.[2]

The myriad ways in which parents influence, shape, and determine their children's worldviews are too numerous and play out on too many levels, to be fully detailed or adequately outlined here. Suffice it to say that having at least one parent who is notably irreligious plants a seed in a child's mind—by way of example, instruction, or both—that irreligion is a legitimate option. As the children grow up, no matter how religious they may become, that seed is always there, inside them, ready to sprout if watered by certain life circumstances or internal questions and doubts. Even if the nonreligious parent "goes along" with the religion of the family, participating fully in church activities, praying with the family around the dinner table, children can still sense their lack of true faith, their subtle skepticism, and their tempered enthusiasm.[3]

Sometimes, of course, the nonreligious parent's secularity isn't subtle, and his or her influence is overt. For a vivid example of how having a nonreligious parent can directly influence a child's later apostasy, consider this wonderfully illustrative recollection from Blanca, age 49. Blanca's father and grandparents were Catholic, and she was raised accordingly. Her mother, however, was a nonbeliever, which clearly affected Blanca's religious socialization:

> When I was seven—when I did my first communion—I had a huge flu. And
> I had a 104 fever. I mean, it was really horrible. I was so sick. And I was so
> bummed that the next day—because of my communion—you know, the pink
> dress and all of that. And I thought that I was not going to be able to do my first

communion. So the next day—I woke up with no fever. And I had prayed and prayed and prayed—I mean … and I really believed that it was an action of God! And I kept saying to my mom, "See! See! He answered my prayers!" and I remember my mom saying, "Yeah, isn't that great." So I went to my communion and I kept saying to everybody, "I'm proof that miracles can happen!" And then my mom finally said to me, "Look—you were loaded with Tylenol, okay?" And I looked at her, like: how dare you? I was SO angry at her. I said, "No! No! Even with the medication, I was feeling better because God wanted me to feel better." And she kept saying, "No." And I hated her for that. But that stuck with me, you know.

Today, Blanca is an atheist.

Most people, however, did not have such clear or distinct memories of a nonreligious parent so unambiguously squelching their childhood faith. For most men and women, having a relatively nonreligious parent was not recalled or described as being significant or overtly problematic. It wasn't characterized as some sort of personal dilemma or source of family conflict. It just was what it was. In fact, most people tended to describe the irreligiosity of one of their parents in a rather off-handed manner, placing little emphasis upon it.

But for Milton and Ali, it was most definitely decisive. For Milton, raised a Roman Catholic in Delaware, and for Ali, raised a Muslim in Saudi Arabia, having an irreligious parent was actually a crucial problem, with secularizing consequences.

Milton is 45 years old. He is currently an adjunct professor of anthropology and is married with two children. For the first 20 years of his life, he enjoyed being Catholic, and he found it meaningful and engaging. He went to a Catholic elementary school, and after his confirmation his commitment only deepened. He collected rosaries and statuettes of saints, he studied church history and theology, and he even wore a scapular—a stringed adornment that you wear under your clothes that hangs over your shoulders, bearing religious images over your chest and back. He was elected president of his church youth group when he was 15 years old. He prayed a lot, went to confession regularly, and he believed in essential Catholic teachings: the virgin birth, the resurrection of Jesus, heaven and hell. And yet, it was his belief in hell, specifically, that would be the first domino to fall. He got stuck on this one, especially as it concerned his father. For Milton had always been taught that those who did not believe correctly and were not good Catholics would be spending eternity in a place of eternal torment and anguish. This didn't sit well with him. For one thing, it just seemed manifestly inhumane that anyone should be subject to endless suffering for merely adhering to a different religion or to no religion at all. But for another thing—and this one was much closer to home—his father was not very active in the Catholic faith. He wasn't opposed to it, per se. He just wasn't all that into it. He often skipped church, and he didn't seem as committed as he should be. This worried Milton. His father was a loving man, a gentle man, a good husband, and a well-liked high school teacher. He just wasn't that religious. For this he might go to hell?

> Dad...was a very moral person. The fact that he didn't always go to church with us...didn't mean that he wasn't a good person. But, of course, at the same time, we're learning catechism—we're learning ideas from the church about the Catholic Church being the "true" church and people who don't accept it are damned to hell, and so forth. So that particular problem, I remember thinking about at a very early age....I mean, that fundamental problem of justice—as simplistic as it is—I remember weighing quite heavily on me. Who's going to hell, and why? And why do they deserve it? And why should my father, if he's such a good person, why should he be risking this? I knew there were people that I thought were good and that—other people that I knew and whose opinions counted—and also thought were good people. So I'm continually grappling with this moral dilemma of salvation and damnation and the justice of that.

By the time Milton had completed his first week of college, he was a confirmed atheist.

Like Milton, Ali could not reconcile his religion with the reality of his mother's less-than-pious identity. Ali is 35 years old. He was born and raised in Saudi Arabia, some 30 miles or so from Mecca. He currently lives in Pasadena, California, where he owns a small but successful company. Although Ali's parents were both Muslim, they were what he described as "secular Muslims." They were thus Muslim mostly in terms of their heritage, upbringing, and identity. Sure, they celebrated various Muslim holidays throughout the year. But they weren't strong believers in God, nor did they necessarily believe that the Qu'ran was divine in nature. They didn't follow all the rules and laws of the Muslim faith. They were modern in their styles and tastes, well educated and Westernized. They lived in a sort of "secularized social bubble" in Saudi Arabia, spending time with like-minded friends who weren't opposed to drinking alcohol at social events, who enjoyed American pop music, who believed in equality between men and women, and were critical of the lack of democracy in Saudi society.

This was Ali's life at home. But school was another story. There, Ali was surrounded by fundamentalist Islam. Of the 13 subjects he was required to take at school, five were solely about religion. He learned to pray, to memorize and recite the Qu'ran, and to follow all the rules and laws of the Wahhabi sect. It was a severe version of Islam:

> *Islam as a religion teaches that if you—like, it's not a questioning religion. It's not a progressive religion. It just isn't—at least the one I got taught. Sure, there's maybe softer versions. But not the one I learned in Saudi Arabia. The one I learned in Saudi Arabia was a very intolerant, very violent Islam. You know, if you change your religion from Islam to another, the version of Islam that I learned had the punishment be death.*
>
> *The way the religion is structured is whoever would kill me, would actually get religious bonus points in the eyes of God. The Islam we learned was not a peaceful Islam. It wasn't a tolerant Islam.*

Many of Ali's friends were devout, as were many of his teachers. He was impressed by their serious piety and tried to emulate it. He began to follow their lead, immersing himself in Islam's ways. And he was good at it. He was eventually selected to be the muezzin for his class—the one who leads/sings the calls to prayer. This was quite an honor. For an extended period of time, he straddled the fence: he immersed himself within the holy world of Islam while at school and among his friends, but he also enjoyed the more secular atmosphere at home. He wanted to be religious, to love God, and to be a pious Muslim in word and deed. But then the harsh reality of Islam came up against the loving reality of his mother:

> I recall one of the times that allowed me to even question all of this doctrine was—at a very young age—a religion teacher was describing, you know, I guess what he called the "good" Muslim woman and the "bad" Muslim woman. His description of the "bad" Muslim woman was a woman who didn't cover her hair and the "good" one being the one who would cover her hair, and obviously her body. The "good" Muslim woman was the one that, for example, shunned drinking alcohol and the "bad" one would, whatever socially or— drink alcohol. He also mentioned fraternizing with men who were not her immediate family—husband or children. So I remember sitting there in class...thinking to myself that this guy, his version of the "bad" Muslim woman—he is describing my mother. I internally and emotionally felt like I had to make a choice over following this doctrine or choosing my mother.... So in that moment, the structure of like what this invisible God in the cloud says is right or wrong had a big question mark on it.... This woman was as good of a human being as I had ever encountered, beyond the fact that I loved her and she was my mother.... So I think that was the moment that this whole Islam business came into question as a pathway to some form of truth.

Today, Ali is a nonbeliever.

RAISING THEIR OWN

What about adult apostates who have kids of their own?[4]

Because apostates have tasted the fruit of religion and found it wanting, they have a distinct vantage point. Now that they are secular, how have they raised their own children? What have they taught them about faith and reason, religion and secularity, God and doubt?

There is a unique worry that faces many apostate parents: how do they impart their values and beliefs to their children without "brainwashing" them? Most apostate parents realize that they initially became religious only because their parents raised them to be religious. While they certainly want to pass on their own secular values, secular opinions, and secular beliefs to their children, they don't want to "commit the same crime" of indoctrinating their kids to think just like them. They'd like their children to come to their own decisions about religion, life, death, and morality—something they themselves weren't allowed to do. Yet, simply by sharing their views about their own secularity— simply by not going to church regularly—how can they avoid influencing their children? It is very difficult. Perhaps impossible. And this is something that religious parents simply don't face, for the most part. For religious parents—especially the strongly devout and heavily involved—it is a joy and a duty to bring up their children in the fold, to teach them the tenets of their religion with earnest devotion, and to do all they can to ensure that their children become enmeshed in their religious tradition. It is just what a good parent ought to do. But for parents who are apostates, there is much more self-doubt when it comes to raising children to be secular or not.[5]

When I asked apostates how they raised their kids, the answers ran the gamut. Some actually wanted their kids to be religiously involved and religiously informed. They wanted them to have experiences similar to those they themselves had as kids, to learn the songs, the prayers, and the stories that had been a part of their own upbringing. If their kids then wanted to later reject that religion as they got older, that would be fine. But they should at least have the experience first. Other parents worked hard to raise their kids without any knowledge or sense of religion whatsoever. They wanted them to be raised in a fully secular home—and if, as they got older, they decided to explore religion, well, that would be their own choice. Most parents, however, haphazardly hovered somewhere between these two approaches, seeking to give their kids some sort of religious experience or immersion, while at the same time making it clear that religion wasn't the be-all and end-all. Most apostate parents are thus quite conflicted.

One man who clearly struggled with the question of how to raise his kids is Victor. A former altar boy, he was raised a strong Catholic, and his wife was as well. But they both rejected religion in their teens. Once they had kids of their own, however, it somehow felt wrong to deprive them of a religious upbringing. And yet, at the same time, Victor and his wife didn't want to have anything to do with formal Roman Catholicism. They ended up going to a local Protestant congregation for a spell, but even that didn't quite work out:

> We tried to go to the Methodist Church for a while, because our neighbor down the street was a good member there and a very interested member. That's where I think the guilt comes in. That you feel like: I was raised with religion and everybody around me says, "You've got to give your kids something. You've got to give them some religion." And I was like, well, why? But that's where the guilt comes in. Are we doing something wrong? Is there some sort of fundamental thing about being a citizen that makes religion mean something to these kids later in life? Or is it just a bunch of dogma that you dump into their brains and let them swim through it, you know? So, we thought: well, it's a family thing to do—go to church on Sundays. So we did it for a while, you know, off and on for a couple of years until we just decided we just couldn't take it anymore.

Have your kids ever come home from school and asked, "What do we believe?" Or "Is there a God?" You ever have that conversation?

> I think they have....I haven't really paid much attention to it. Wendy explains it to them some way as "people are people and they believe different things." I have to admit, I'm probably harsh on religion. I've said I don't have any use for it....I wonder: when you're raised religious, then you

don't have religion—and when you were raised without religion, do you crave it later? I don't know. I don't know.

Beatrice, age 39, shared her own struggles as an apostate parent:

My father is really big on "faith is a gift." And he says to me, "It makes me so sad that you have lost your faith because I really do think that it is important for your children to be raised having faith in something." So I think—and what I did, too—and I did this purely for him, and I actually struggle with it because—and I don't think I would do it today—but I had both my kids baptized Catholic. Purely because he would not let it go. It was something he was so adamant about and asking me about and it was affecting our relationship. So I just said, screw it, okay, I'll do it.... With Eve, my daughter, she asked me when she was probably three or four years old—what is God and who is God and what is heaven? I remember—and I'd still do it in this way—I put it in the context of some people believe that there is a God and He is looking down on you all the time and watching you and protecting you and helping you choose right from wrong. I don't think at the time I said, "I don't believe in this," but I did say, "and if that's what you believe, if that's what you want to believe then that's perfectly okay."... Then, for some reason, when she was five...I don't know why I did this, but I bought a children's Bible. I thought, well, she's asking about God, she's asking about Jesus, we celebrate Christmas so maybe it's time to just, you know, share like stories from the Bible. So I bought this children's Bible and we would read a few stories and she would say, did this really happen? I said, "You know, some people believe this really did happen, but some people don't." I think at that time I said, "I don't believe that this really happened, but that doesn't mean we can't learn from the stories that we're reading."

Whereas Beatrice did allow certain elements of religion into her kids' life, and even affirmed a belief in heaven and bought her daughter a children's Bible, Chuck, age 36, has tried his hardest to shield his daughter from anything even remotely smacking of Christianity. Chuck was a strongly believing Pentecostal in his youth but has been a nonbeliever since his twenties. He still harbors a fair amount of bitterness toward religion, and he thinks that it can actually be harmful to kids. When it came to his four-year-old daughter, he had this recollection:

> *My wife and I made a very conscious decision. For me, if you were to ask me, like, what's your primary value? I would say liberty. . . . I believe that people should be free to be as they wish. So for me, it was a really important thing for my daughter not to have the idea of God growing up—as much as possible. So we have really, really tried to keep even the notion out of her head for now. She goes to preschool at the Congregational Church, and when we went there to the interview, I said, "Look, we're non-Christian and I know this is a church, but I know this thing is supposed to be separate." And they assured us up and down there's no religious stuff here. And, of course, in practice they do. I don't really know how much of it she gets there. She hasn't come back to me yet and asked anything about what is God.*

What do you think you'll say when she does?

> *I think for me the most important thing is I don't want her to grow up with the idea that there's a being watching over her at all times and monitoring her and what she does. I want her to feel free to be good. . . . My mom is still very religious and when she comes out, I have to talk with her. . . . I remember when McKenzie was little—my mom saying something like, "Oh, God doesn't like that" or something like that [laughs]. I remember having to afterwards take my mom aside and say, "Look, I don't want you doing that."*

* * *

Countless studies have detailed the many ways in which family life determines and shapes religion and how religion in turn affects and infuses family life. What is missing, however, is research on the ways in which family life is related to secularity and the rejection of religion. What I have offered is a mere scratching of the surface—a limited glimpse at the very real phenomenon of irreligiosity related to family dynamics. From the conversations I have had with apostates about their parents and their kids, I can confidently argue that apostasy is clearly related to a lack of religious enthusiasm in one's parents (or at least one parent) and that apostates themselves struggle with how to raise their own kids religiously (or secularly) in ways that religious parents don't. And if I had to make a prediction, I'd bet that the children of apostates are much more likely to remain secular themselves later in life. In the blunt words of social psychologist Bob Altemeyer:

> If you (correctly) believe that very religious offspring tend to come from very religious upbringings, you can see why a nonreligious background can lead to nonbelief. Socialization usually works.[6]

10

✧

How and Why People Reject Religion

What causes certain people living in the United States in the first decade of the twenty-first century to reject religion? How does it happen?

To begin with, the overwhelming majority of those whom I interviewed described their apostasy as a gradual process. While there were perhaps a handful of atypical individuals who had experienced certain immediate, faith-shattering "A-ha!" moments, most did not. Rather, their rejection of religion was an incremental process, taking place over a period of three to five years, sometimes longer.[1] Second, it was rare for someone to pin his or her apostasy on one specific cause. More commonly, people said that their apostasy was the result of numerous factors, working in conjunction with one another, steadily compounding over time. Third, apostasy does not always result in the embracing of absolute, convinced atheism. Roughly half of my interviewees ended up as confirmed, steadfast nonbelievers in God. But others labeled themselves agnostics. Some just sort of casually said, "I don't know what I believe." Others said that although they no longer believed in the God of their earlier religion, they still did believe in "something out there"—an unnamable, undefinable, but somehow spiritual entity of some sort. And a handful of people even claimed to believe in God—but their own personally constructed, individually conceived, unique, nonbiblical version of God. And there were of course some people who simply preferred to label themselves "spiritual" and leave it at that. Some people resisted a label altogether. For example, Stanley, who is 38 years old and grew up in Texas, and who once was a Bible-believing minister-in-training but who rejected Christianity and lost his faith many years ago, didn't want to label himself in any particular way:

> I would say I'm definitely not a religious person, but . . . I don't feel that I need to call myself an atheist really, because to me that feels like I have something I've got to prove. . . . So to me, I guess I could maybe say that I feel there's a part of me that could be spiritual, but I don't like that term because it's connected with religion. I guess in the end, I would say I know there's aspects of my experience that I cannot explain through logic and reason and I just kind of leave it at that.

Regardless of where apostates have ended up—atheist, agnostic, unsure, spiritual, or something else—what all those I interviewed shared was a very clear and obvious distancing from their religion in terms of belief, adherence, identification, membership, and/or participation, and for the majority, an outright loss or rejection thereof.

As you can imagine, when you ask so many individuals *why* they lost their faith and/or left their religion, you get many, many answers. Some were quite idiosyncratic. For example, one woman claimed that it was solely about birth control; she wanted to be on it, her religion said no, and so she left her religion—case closed. Another woman actually "tested" her religion to see if it made any qualitative difference in her life; she spent about two years believing in God, praying regularly, attending church and a Bible study class, and then she spent about one year not believing in God, not praying, and abstaining from any religious involvement. She found that life was simply better as a secular person, so she's been secular—a convinced atheist, in fact—ever since. There was one man who visited a children's hospital, saw all the children there dying of cancer, and was so saddened that his belief in God withered fairly soon after. One woman read *The God Delusion* by Richard Dawkins, and "that was that." For another man it was dinosaurs. He learned about them as a kid, didn't see how they fit into all the Bible stories he was learning at church, and subsequently developed a skeptical attitude towards religion. One man started to feel alienated from his religion when the words "God Hates Fags" were spray-painted on a wall at the small, Midwestern Christian college he was attending. Although not gay himself, such religious-inspired intolerance opened his eyes, causing him to look at the negative aspects of his religion, where before he had only seen the positive. In short, almost every apostate had his or her own particular story, with his or her own personal reasons. As Colin Campbell has observed, "the factors which actually give rise to the irreligious response are likely to be as complex and as diverse as the causes of religious commitment."[2]

But there were definitely some common, oft-cited reasons that came up again and again. Here are the nine most typical, most pervasive, or most often mentioned reasons given by apostates in accounting for their rejection of religion.

1. PARENTS

"Religious socialization," notes sociologist Stephen Hunt, "is most likely to be successful when parents are openly committed to their religion."[3] But when only one parent is religious and the other one is lukewarm or an outright nonbeliever, the likelihood of apostasy for the children of such a couple is increased. My findings confirm what social scientists have observed for decades, that children are heavily influenced by the parents, especially when it comes to their religious identity—or the subsequent rejection thereof.[4]

2. EDUCATION

Elizabeth was easily one of the most religious individuals included in this study. Pentecostal Christianity pervaded nearly every aspect of her life for many years. But then she took a sociology class at a local community college. The result of this foray into secular education was dramatic:

> *I learned about cultures, and I learned about people, and I learned how and why we do things and why we don't do things and—just conforming . . . and I was hearing what he was saying and it was just kinda rocking my world . . . my world had expanded suddenly. . . . And I would be overwhelmed. And I loved it. And it made me kinda scared, because I realized that maybe there was more to the world than I had thought or had been allowed to know. I would go home and tell my roommates—who were my best friends and all of us, you know, we all went to church together. I would say, "Guess what I talked about today?" and Ruthie and Clark—my friends that went to Bible College—looked at me. And they were my closest, most dear friends. They looked at me and said, "You need to stop going to that class. Don't go to class anymore, Elizabeth. It's ruining your faith." And when they said that to me, I realized that that was wrong and that was exactly what I needed to be doing is going to class and learning.*

Elizabeth eventually did lose her faith—and her best friends.

Many of the men and women I talked to found that going to college made them look at the world differently, forced them to ask questions that they had never wanted or even thought to ask, and caused them to scrutinize their own values and beliefs. Elizabeth's story is not uncommon, and previous research has consistently correlated increased educational attainment with increased secularity and apostasy.[5]

3. MISFORTUNE

For some people, when they experience loss or pain in their lives, it leads them to question God's goodness, even God's existence. The untimely death of a parent, a bitter divorce, or even the loss of a beloved pet—such difficult experiences can ignite skepticism. And when people who have been devoutly religious experience such difficult loss or pain, they can have difficulty understanding how it could be happening to them. Their confusion is all the more confounded when their prayers go unheeded. Rather than cling to God, they feel forsaken. While most people embrace or cling to their religion in the face of personal difficulties, some do just the opposite.

4. OTHER CULTURES, OTHER RELIGIONS

Caleb, age 61, was a strongly believing and proudly active Mormon for most of his life. He was also a great organ player. Because of his musical skills, he was sought out by many congregations in his community, and he was offered many gigs.

About 20 years ago, I started substituting in other churches and they paid me....I was regularly playing for other churches, on their staff under contract. Which meant every Sunday I'm hearing another point of view. I was playing for a Lutheran church...and the associate pastor—every Sunday he gave the sermon and he would work into it somewhere that only Missouri Synod Lutherans were going to heaven and everyone else was going to hell.... This just amazed me. Infuriated me. I'm sitting up at the organ and listening to this guy just spew this: "We're the only ones on the bus and everybody else is getting off before it." It infuriated me, and one day it hit me why it made me so angry: it's because I knew it was really the Mormons that were going all the way to the end of the line and everybody else was getting off the bus and how dare he say there's anyone else! That really shifted my paradigm, because then I realize everybody really said that. The Adventists said it's wearing jewelry that sends you to hell and worshipping on Sunday. Jehovah's Witnesses—it's celebrating holidays and birthdays. This is the list that guarantees entrance to heaven and this is the list that sends you to hell—and everybody had their list! How could I be so lucky as to get the right one?

Although there were many reasons why Caleb eventually left the Church of Latter-Day Saints—prominent among them was his support for gay rights—his regular exposure to other beliefs played a big part. Attending worship services of numerous Protestant denominations, all with their own particular doctrines and relatively unique emphases, forced Caleb to question his own. Everyone else was sure that they were right. So was he. But they couldn't all be right. So might he be wrong?

For some people, it is moving to a new country and being exposed to new ways of life that makes them question their beliefs. For others, it is experiencing or becoming acquainted with other religions. For still others, it is simply taking a class in which they learn about other religions, other cultures. But the underlying dynamic is always the same: experiencing, witnessing, or learning about other people who do things differently, believe different things, and/or hold different outlooks on life can stir up a process of critical self-reflection that can be potentially corrosive to one's long-held religious convictions.[6]

5. FRIENDS, COLLEAGUES, LOVERS

If it isn't our parents that affect and influence us, then it is other people who are closest to us. Take the example of Henry, age 41, who grew up in a working-class suburb in Orange County, New Jersey. His mother was a hairdresser and his father was a plumber. Both parents were devout; theirs was a strongly religious Irish Catholic home. Henry was an ardent, earnest believer for the first two decades of his life. In his teens he ventured out of his Catholic circle and meandered into the vibrant Evangelical youth movement some of his friends were participating in. Henry prayed constantly, studied his Bible constantly, and attended church two or three times a week. Christianity was at the core of his being:

> *I really believed it. I was buying everything. . . . I definitely believed in Jesus, that he died for us and the life after death . . . and I was always worried about the devil. . . . Hell was always a worry.*

Today, Henry defines himself as an "explicit, outspoken atheist." What happened?

I was 20 and I got my first job in video games—it was a contract to work 7 days a week, 12 hours a day, and fairly decent money. I was a young gun right out of community college. It was kind of an informal atmosphere. I would be working at like three in the morning with this zany yet brilliant engineer . . . and we would have these conversations and we got along great. The guy had an awesome personality: very smart, very funny, very generous. . . . He first questioned my faith—because I was an ardent believer still. I remember he was bringing up various things like basically, the arguments on evil, for one of the big ones. I'm talking about why is there so much suffering in the world if there's a God and all that stuff. How could you believe that? "It's silly, haven't you ever thought about maybe there's not a God." So anyway, he got me to start thinking that I was wrong—or that I had to check my Bible and prove him wrong. So I was really annoyed by that. Eventually the conversation ended, we did our work, and I went home and read my Bible and checked out a couple things. . . . I remember thinking: he's right. You know, whatever he was saying—it's hard to remember the details—but I remember what he was saying about certain things in the Bible that God did this or killed these people or had them killed. You know, some guy got killed for picking up sticks on the Sabbath or whatever. I remember verifying it and going: "Oh wow, this is crazy, I never hear about this in church." . . . I remember there was this conflict and, as a believer, I remember thinking that "this is bad." You know: "I am not supposed to doubt because I'm going to go to hell and I'm going to anger God." So while I was busy unraveling religion, I was also, as a believer, afraid that I was being unraveled and not wanting to have that conflict. . . . So I literally—it was like this battle between good and evil in my brain. At some point, you know, we talked more and I started thinking that I was just wrong, that someone had just lied to me and that my parents didn't really know any better—they just told me what they believed. . . .

At some point it just clicked. It's really weird, but I was sitting in my room realizing, as I was reading my Bible, realizing in almost from one minute to the next—I was an atheist. I actually went through a small agnostic phase—it was only a few days, though. A lot of people talk about years of de-conversion. But I remember at one point saying, "I'm an atheist and I don't believe this." And I rejected it. . . .

And here's another thing I have to mention. This is the first atheist I ever met—that I knowingly met—that discussed religion with me. I had never been exposed to an atheist who was actually questioning my religion before.

So this is the first time you even had these kinds of debates?

> *Right, THE first time I really had this debate. Yeah, absolutely, because the kids that I hung around with were religious, you know, and I never encountered that before. . . . But this is somebody I liked who I didn't know was an atheist and it was my boss, right. I thought he was like one of the coolest guys and they were paying me ridiculous amounts of money and just had a lot of respect for him and his intellect and him as a person, how generous he was.*

So it is possible to be argued out of one's faith?
Absolutely.

But it wasn't just the specific arguments that de-converted Henry. It was also the fact that the arguments themselves came out of the mouth of someone he worked with day after day and night after night, someone he liked, someone he respected and admired. For many people, having a close connection or positive relationship with someone who is nonreligious can be a powerfully influential factor in their apostasy. Indeed, Henry's own apostasy had a ripple affect:

> *Later on, my mom—it took me eight years—she actually became an atheist. We actually went to an atheist party together and met a bunch of other atheists.*

A significant amount of research has shown the degree to which one's social intimates can affect and influence one's own religious choices and commitments. The same dynamic is at play within the realm of secular life; it is often one's social intimates that can spur and direct one's irreligiosity and eventual apostasy.[7]

6. POLITICS

Extensive research has revealed that the more religious you are, the likelier you will be to hold conservative, right-wing political views—and conversely, the more conservative and right-wing you are politically, the greater is the likelihood that you will be strongly religious. In the United States, strong religiosity and strong conservative politics go hand in hand. There are, of course, exceptions to this rule; strongly religious African Americans, for example, still tend to vote overwhelmingly for Democrats. But this glaring exception aside, when taking into account national averages, strongly religious Americans—when compared to the less religious or irreligious—are much more likely to support the death penalty; support draconian punishment for prisoners; support the policies of former President George W. Bush; support the war in Iraq; support the governmental use of torture; oppose gay marriage and gay rights; oppose welfare spending that helps society's unfortunate, hungry, or disabled; and oppose regulations to protect the environment.[8]

What all of this means is that religiously active Americans whose politics are left-wing or progressive may experience a sense of alienation. Indeed, sociologists Michael Hout and Claude Fischer have argued that much of the recent increase in nonreligious Americans can be attributed to people being turned off by the political activism of the religious right, and seeking to distance themselves from religiously linked political conservatism.[9]

Many religious people who support gay marriage, oppose the war in Iraq, support protecting the environment, fear the likes of Sarah Palin, or simply identify as vegetarians are apt to feel some conflict with what they are hearing at church or around their family's dinner table. Some simply keep their progressive political leanings to themselves and continue to be actively religious. But for others, their progressive political convictions are too strong to be stifled or denied, and they subsequently feel unable or unwilling to continue participating in their politically conservative religious culture.

That's what happened to Nicole, age 19. Although she was totally immersed in her church for years and was a strong believer since early childhood, she came to realize at a certain point that her left-wing political leanings were too sharply at odds with her religious milieu:

> *War issues, death penalty, abortion, gay rights especially—I didn't want the*
> *church to tell me how to vote. I just disagreed so much with how they wouldn't*
> *allow gays to marry, how men are so dominant in that church society ... even*
> *in high school ... my viewpoints were always just so—I was the most liberal*
> *person there, and I'm not even that liberal.*

Today, Nicole identifies as nonreligious.

7. SEX

An essential feature of most religions, according to founding sociologist Max Weber, is a deep hostility toward sex. And if the orientation toward sex is not quite one of deep hostility, almost every religion still maintains and seeks to impose some form of relatively restrictive sexual regulation that delineates who one can have sex with, as well as when, where, and how.[10]

There were basically three key ways in which issues of sex and sexuality were contributing factors in many people's rejection of religion. The first had to do with desire. Some people, as they hit their teenage years or early twenties, found themselves wanting to have sex. But this desire was flatly condemned by their religion.[11] They thus felt themselves caught between what their bodies and hearts so desperately wanted to do, and what their minister or their God so stridently wanted them not to do. Many people are able to successfully deny or sublimate their sexual urges and continue to do their minister's and their God's bidding. Many others live lives of hypocrisy: secretly engaging in sexual activity while simultaneously upholding a religious front. But still others take a third route: they choose to engage in sexual activity, and they subsequently let their church attendance—and even faith—dissipate. This was the route taken by many apostates that I interviewed.[12] A second way in which sex can contribute toward apostasy has to do with guilt. Many religions spend a lot of time and energy making their adherents feel shame and guilt about sexual urges and desires. Sex becomes heavily associated with sin, uncleanliness, and moral depravity. Religiously inspired feelings of shame and guilt can be so strongly internalized that when some men and women finally have sex— even within marriage—these feelings linger and are hard to shake.[13] This emotional linkage of healthy sexual desire/experience with guilt/shame can leave a bitter taste in some people's mouths. They came to resent what they had been taught, and the way it made them feel. Some distanced themselves from religion. Finally, there is the matter of homosexuality. There is simply no question that being gay or lesbian can strongly contribute toward someone's apostasy. Gays and lesbians learn early on that their sexual identity is unwelcome, unacceptable, and downright unholy. So many leave—and they go on to embrace secular values and secular worldviews that confirm and celebrate who they are, rather than deny and deride. Indeed, Thomas Linneman and Margaret Clendenen report that homosexuals and bisexuals are nearly three times more likely to be atheist or agnostic than heterosexuals.[14]

8. SATAN AND HELL

"Whoso disbelieveth in Allah...whoso findeth ease in disbelief: On them is wrath from Allah. Theirs will be an awful doom." So declares the Qu'ran.[15] As for unbelievers within the Christian tradition, they shall be cast into a "fiery lake of burning sulfur."[16] And Satan, according to Mormon scriptures, "cheateth their souls, and leadeth them away carefully down to hell...he grasps them with his awful chains, from whence there is no deliverance. Yea, they are grasped with death, and hell; and death, and hell, and the devil, and all that have been seized therewith...must go into the place prepared for them, even a lake of fire and brimstone, which is endless torment."[17]

Fear can be one of the most powerful motivators of human behavior.[18] And many religions—particularly conservative or traditional versions of Christianity and Islam—contain a heavy element of fear. They teach that there is a Devil, that there are demons, and that hell awaits the disobedient. Such teachings motivate many people to stay within their religious fold and to be faithful followers of a God they believe will protect and save them. Of course, some people within these religious traditions don't feel the same level of fear. They enjoy other aspects of their religion, don't worry too much about Satan or hell, and are motivated in their faith not by fear, but by love, hope, or compassion.[19] But for many people, the Devil and his fiery hell cannot be ignored.

Many of the people I interviewed, particularly those who had been raised in conservative Protestant denominations or strongly Catholic households, had been taught to fear Satan and hell. And they did. And this fear remained an ugly, damaging, disturbing element of their lives for many years. As they got older, they began to resent it, hate it, and eventually question it. Such teachings and beliefs can, for some people, produce long-term negative feelings, entrenched discomfort, and prolonged despair. And some people with such experiences, at some point, just want to get away from the source of those feelings, namely their religion.

9. MALFEASANCE OF RELIGIOUS ASSOCIATES

Most religious people, at one time or another, come into contact with unsavory people who should not, given their outward religiosity and ostensibly piety, be so unsavory. Perhaps it is one of their fellow congregants. Or maybe it is their priest, pastor, or minister. For many of the men and women whom I interviewed, their withdrawal from religion was spurred in large part by religious people that they knew, or knew of, who acted in such a way as to create feelings of unease, disappointment, or repugnance.

For Rachel, it was the immorality of her own parents. Her folks were strongly religious, and yet they fought a lot. In fact, when she was a teenager, Rachel once had to call the police in a last-ditch attempt to stop her father from beating her mother mercilessly. The domestic violence Rachel witnessed for years made her lose tremendous respect for both of her parents—her father for perpetrating it, and her mother for continuing to live with it. It caused her to question her parents' morality and the religion it was supposedly based upon. Additionally, they were Jehovah's Witnesses, and one of the most decisive blows to her religiosity was when Rachel's parents acted in a way that she viewed as grossly negligent:

> A huge part of me basically de-converting was when my brother was born and almost died—and my parents refused to allow him a blood transfusion. They would rather he had died than receive a blood transfusion. That was a huge part of my basically de-converting at that point.

Today, Rachel is an atheist.

Reasons Are Not Necessarily Causes

As much of this book has documented, apostates can readily articulate the varied reasons behind their rejection of religion. The most common reasons have been summarized above. But subjective reasons are not necessarily objective causes. That is, while the reasons apostates give as the underlying factors in their rejection of religion are personally true and subjectively real causes of apostasy for them, in the unfolding of their own personal lives, these same reasons are not necessarily things that would independently, objectively—in and of themselves—cause apostasy to occur for anyone or everyone.

Consider Rachel, discussed above. Her parents' reluctance to give her baby brother a blood transfusion kindled her eventual apostasy. But most kids raised as Jehovah's Witnesses are fully aware of their religion's prohibition on blood transfusions.

Many of them have had firsthand experiences of the implications of this prohibition. And yet most do not subsequently become apostates. Furthermore, many people have had parents who fought a lot and even beat one another up on occasion, as did Rachel's. But this usually causes the children of such a hostile union to cling even more strongly to religious faith, not to reject it.

Let me give another specific example of how reasons for apostasy are not the same thing as causes thereof.

In her teenage years, Geraldine experienced an intense inner conflict between wanting to have sex and wanting to be a good Christian. Throughout high school, it was the latter urge that prevailed. But once she started college, she just couldn't stifle her sexual desires any longer. She started having sex, and her religiosity quickly withered. Thus, "wanting to have premarital sex" was cited by Geraldine, unapologetically, as *the* significant reason underlying her apostasy. But here's the thing: while Geraldine's desire to have sex was a subjectively true reason behind her apostasy, it is not, in and of itself, an objective, independent cause of apostasy. If it were, religion would have long vanished from societies. Most people have sexual urges throughout their teenage years. Most people continue to have strong sexual urges as young adults. And most people—just like Geraldine—will eventually go on to satisfy those urges prior to getting married. But the fact remains that most people who experience strong sexual urges as young adults, and even go on to act on those urges, do not also go on to simultaneously reject their religion.[20] They don't stop believing in God. They still go to church, they still pray, they stay within their religious fold. Thus, while we can validly and accurately acknowledge that "wanting to have premarital sex" was a very real reason underlying Geraldine's apostasy, we must simultaneously recognize and admit that it is not necessarily an objective, independent cause of apostasy in its own right.

The same can be said for every single reason broached by my interviewees. Most people who experience the untimely death of a parent do not go on to become irreligious. Most people who experience a painful divorce do not become secular. Most people—even those who have a mean pastor or a hypocritical coreligionist, or who maintain divergent political views from the majority of the other individuals in their congregation, or who live abroad for a year among a different culture, or who take a world religions class, or who have a parent who is not all that religious, or who find that their prayers go unanswered, or who were raised to fear the devil—do not all become apostates. Even most gays and lesbians will choose to continue within their religious traditions and simply ignore or rationalize the lack of acceptance of homosexuality therein. Others might go on to find an alternative religious tradition that accepts them for who they are.[21] But the point is that they don't all become godless or even secular.[22]

The best one can say—the most one can safely conclude when it comes to the various subjective reasons summarized in this chapter—is that they may *increase the likelihood* of a person's eventual rejection of religion. A person who experiences the premature death of a parent is *more likely* to question God, and to eventually decide to become an atheist, than a person who has not suffered such a loss. Certainly someone who grew up with a secular or at least religiously unenthusiastic parent will be *more likely* to lose faith than someone whose parents were both earnestly devout. People who experience a different culture will be *more likely* to come to question the eternal truths of their religion than those who never get out of their own social or religious milieu.

In sum, a sociological theory of apostasy must remain humble. All that can be asserted with confidence is that a variety of life circumstances, personal experiences, and/or social dynamics can increase the likelihood that certain individuals will go on to reject their religion. But there is no one single "thing"—be it an experience, event, relationship, and so on—that always, in and of itself, *causes* apostasy. All the factors I've mentioned can increase the chances or likelihood that a person will reject religion. And when several of them occur in a given person's life simultaneously, they become cumulatively corrosive to religious faith.

In truth, while subjective reasons for apostasy are easily discernible, objective causes are much more difficult to uncover, and perhaps impossible to prove, given the many complex factors at play in any single human's life.

Secular by Nature?

There is one final issue worthy of consideration. It is an issue that haunted my year and a half of conducting in-depth interviews. It has to do with the possibility of whether or not some people are simply predisposed toward irreligion. They just *are* secular, in their core. I say that this matter "haunted" me because sociologists, by and large, generally don't place much emphasis on "natural" tendencies or innate predispositions when trying to explain people's beliefs or behaviors. But as I listened to apostate after apostate, I often found myself wondering if it might be possible that some people are simply secular by nature.

While most apostates had explicit reasons for their loss of faith and/or rejection of religion, some did not. Their apostasy "just happened." It was an unavoidable outcome of an inner, "natural" secularity. Such people described their loss of faith and rejection of religion as something that just couldn't be helped. It was an inevitable, almost uncontrollable emergence of something that they had always felt inside of them, as part of "who they always were." Such individuals had often tried their hardest to be religious, they had done their best to have faith, and they had possessed an earnest, genuine will to feel God in a way that they had been raised to. But in the end, such things just didn't resonate, didn't jive, didn't work. They didn't register with who they were, at root. Their apostasy was thus something that they "recognized" or "accepted" or "admitted to"—rather than something chosen or preferred.

Consider Eugene. Born and raised a Baptist, he became a Methodist in his early twenties, and then he eventually became an atheist. Here's how he describes that last transformation:

Sometime in my late twenties—I'll say 27, 28 years old—I was going by myself to a Methodist church in the suburbs of Maryland. I really enjoyed it. We had an excellent minister who gave great talks. But it finally just dawned on me, you know: "I don't think I really believe this. I think I have to just admit it. I'm a nonbeliever, I'm an atheist. There's no point in trying to pretend any- more and fool myself. I can't fool myself." Then I realized why I was always uncomfortable as a kid, because I think I was making myself believe because I was supposed to believe it.

So, I stopped going then. I finally told my wife. I said, "I'm really not going to go back. I don't think I'm a believer." She took it well. She is a real genuine Catholic—she may have been disappointed, but she's very flexible. That's when I came to admit it to myself. And so I never went back....

It was a light bulb that went on. It isn't that I decided that I was going to be an atheist. I just discovered I was.

Eugene "discovered" that he was an atheist. He didn't decide. His secularity was just something that was inside of him. He did not reject religion for any of the common reasons outlined in the previous chapter—it wasn't about sex, or parental influence, or educational experiences, or being influenced by friends or family, or having political differences with his coreligionists. It just was a matter of coming to terms with what had always been part of him: a genuine inability to believe what he was raised to believe.

I heard similar stories.

Scott, age 36, was born and raised in North Dakota in a very tight-knit Lutheran community. He was religiously active throughout his childhood and was a leader in his church youth group. But he always felt like something was different about his religiosity, fervent though it was. Something was off, somehow. But of course, growing up in a small, rural religious community, there were no words to describe his inner orientation. No con- cepts or labels. He didn't even know what it was until later in life. It was agnosticism:

I think I've always felt agnostic. But I didn't know what that was as a child....

So I struggled with that as a kid, because I thought that was the devil telling me—to try to get me to think other ideas. I would often hear relatives say, "Scott, you ask too many questions. Some of the answers you may hear when you talk to other religions. They may tickle your ears, but that means it sounds good, it doesn't mean it's the truth. So that's the devil trying to tickle your ears." They were always saying: "Be careful who you hang out with, be careful about talking with people from other religions because they might try to get you to switch to theirs." So they would say if you have some Muslim friends or some Jewish friends: "You've got to be careful unless you can convince them to become a Christian. You've got to be careful, otherwise they're going to try to get you to be like them." I thought, what would be so wrong with that? They're nice people. I'd want to be like them....

So I always felt that I was agnostic, but I never really knew what that word was until I was about 19 in college. A friend said it, and the emotion that went through me when he said the word was really scared. I mean, a friend that's an agnostic. "Isn't that like an atheist or...?" I didn't know what it was. And he said it just means that you don't know. My friend Marlon said that, and he said it just means that you're not so vain that you think you have the only answer. It's another way of being in the middle. When he said that, I thought: oh my God, I've always been that.

One of the most common metaphors people employed in describing their apostasy was that it was akin to "coming out" as a homosexual. Such people said that they had tried their hardest to be religious—and they had even convinced themselves for a spell that they did have faith—but in the end, they just couldn't deny their internal irreligiosity any longer, and they had to simply admit and embrace the atheism or agnosticism that seemed to be at the core of their being. For some people, this resulted in rejection from friends and tears from parents. But there was simply nothing they could do about it. They couldn't fake it anymore. They couldn't pretend to believe what they didn't believe, and they couldn't pretend to find deep personal meaning in creeds, rituals, services, or experiences that really had little if any significance for them.[23]

Though much more data on this front are sorely needed, one highly plausible overarching explanation of apostasy is that it is social *and* psychological, entailing a combination of innate, psychological factors triggered or unlocked by certain sociological factors. That is, some apostates may be people who have an internal predisposition toward secularity, which then blossoms or emerges in the wake of certain decisive experiences in their social lives—personally secularizing catalysts—such as those outlined in this chapter.[24]

Conclusion

As a social-psychological rule of thumb, it is hard to beat this one: most people, most of the time, conform.[1]

But clearly there are important exceptions, and apostasy is one of them. The phenomenon of apostasy reveals, if nothing more, just how truly complex and stubbornly unpredictable human beings are. While most people accept and adopt the religious worldview of their parents, their community, their culture, and their society, some don't. Apostasy is thus strong evidence of the undeniable significance and importance of individuality, variability, and human agency. Despite the sociological fact that most of us go along with and internalize the values, norms, traditions, beliefs, and worldviews of those who raise us and those who surround us, we are not all cookie-cutter replicas of our families or peer groups or congregational cultures. Socialization, social forces, peer pressure, and active as well as latent mechanisms that promote religious conformity have their undeniable limits. They do not mold or pierce us all in the same way or to the same degree; in some instances, they may even be defied or rejected.[2]

APOSTASY IN SOCIETAL CONTEXT

Although it is a personal process with undeniable psychological components, the rejection of religion is always culture-bound, playing out in specific social settings that greatly color and inform the phenomenon. "Irreligion," writes Colin Campbell, "can only be specific within a given social and cultural context."[3] This keen assertion is readily applicable to apostasy. The dynamics, processes, and underlying causes of the personal rejection of religion will differ markedly from society to society. In some cultures, apostasy is a major move, a deviant act, a risk—personal, professional, and/or political. However, in other cultures, apostasy is fairly common, ordinary, and of relatively little social consequence. For example, in my previous research, I studied secularity in Denmark and Sweden—two of the least religious countries in the world—where apostasy is literally a nonissue. Almost no one I spoke to had any dramatic stories of their loss of faith or rejection of religion. Hardly anyone spoke of any prolonged struggles or inner turmoil in their development as secular men and women. Most people, in all honesty, couldn't even remember when they stopped believing.

It was quite the opposite here in the United States. For many Americans, their rejection of religion and/or loss of faith was a big deal, personally and socially. They had a lot to say about it. And this difference between secular Scandinavians and secular Americans clearly has to do with the fact that the United States is arguably the most religious democracy within the Western world. Clearly, the broader social context is significant. In a relatively irreligious society such as Denmark, the personal rejection of religion is simply no big deal. But in the United States, where religion is vibrant and pervasive, apostasy is more controversial, more deviant, and thus personally more intense and dramatic. In Scandinavia, secularity is the norm, so individuals who choose faith and live religious lives are actually the odd, unusual ones. In contrast, in the United States, it is those who lose their faith and reject religion who are different, atypical, or special. The point is simply that there can be no single, grand, universal explanation or theory of apostasy that transcends time or place. Rather, apostasy is always culture-bound, and thus it is quite different from society to society, depending on the strength and flavor of religion therein.

RELIGION IS NOT UNIVERSAL OR NECESSARY

Another important lesson is that obviously many people, from various walks of life, can live without religion—in fact, prefer as much. This bald fact strongly counters the notion that all people—*as* people—are somehow intrinsically religious or that religion is some sort of necessary, universal, or inextricable component of the human condition. Despite the glaring fact that many countries have experienced significant waves of secularization over the course of the twentieth century, some sociologists of religion continue to theorize about religion as though it is inherent to the human experience.[4] Paul Froese argues that religion is an "essential aspect of the human condition," that God beliefs "lie at the core of human understanding," and that religious belief is universal and essentially unalterable.[5] Reginald Bibby suggests that religious needs are constant, "essential needs" of humanity, similar to the need for food![6]

Apostasy may be rare, but it is nonetheless a plain and persistent social reality.[7] It has been present for thousands of years in one form or another, since the earliest philosophical musings were ever written down.[8] Past documentation of apostasy throughout history, along with more recent studies such as my own, should render suspect assertions about religion being universally necessary or essential to the human experience. The sooner we recognize that religion can be—and frequently is—freely rejected by all sorts of men and women, the sooner our understanding of the human condition will improve.[9] We need to simply accept that some men and women find that life is better, freer, richer, or more honest without faith in God and/or religious involvement. Such individuals are not sociopathic, maladjusted, or "unnatural."

THE APOSTATE PERSONALITY

What are apostates like, then, as people? While some may be angry, alienated, confused, or despondent, the vast majority of people I interviewed did not display these characteristics in any apparent way. Well, maybe some anger, here and there—especially when critiquing objectionable aspects of religion or remembering bad experiences in relation to religion.[10] But by and large, nearly all of the apostates I interviewed seemed to be good, kind, solid men and women. They appeared to be relatively happy, self-assured, well-functioning, articulate, ethical, and decent. Of course, I can't *prove* this. I did not administer any standard personality tests to my informants. All I did, quite frankly, was conduct lengthy conversations with nearly 90 people. To be sure, these conversations were structured so as to maximize the amount of information gleaned; they were generally quite detailed, in-depth, and more often than not, thoughtfully rendered. In most of these interviews, people opened themselves up quite a bit, sharing memories, feelings, thoughts, theories, opinions, regrets, joys, and values. Having conducted so many in-depth, formal interviews of this nature with so many people who were once religious but are no longer left me with some powerfully lasting impressions. And if I had to draw up a sort of generalized portrait—an ideal-typical sketch of what apostates are like—I would include the following details.

Apostates are courageous. "There is a bravery," writes John Allen Paulos, "associated with disbelief and honest doubt."[11] For many individuals, their loss of faith was frightening, emotionally and psychologically, and yet they had to admit and accept their loss of faith, despite the consequences. It takes a fair amount of nerve and guts to openly reject something that is extremely important to one's parents or grandparents or friends, to choose not to participate in something that much of one's community or society deems as noble, to assert one's lack of faith in a world populated by people of faith.[12] And sometimes the stakes of apostasy can be quite high, particularly within fundamentalist circles or strongly religious societies.[13] Apostates are also bright.[14] Inquisitiveness, intellectualism, academic engagement, and/or a love of reading were common traits among most of the men and women in this study. Apostates are also keenly moral; those who have rejected religion actively desire a world of fairness, kindness, goodness, and justice. Apostates are also relatively individualistic and self-reliant. Although they perhaps miss the comfort of community that came with their earlier religious involvement, they don't feel the need any longer to belong to a community of believers given their own lack of belief; they aren't quite comfortable in religious or social organizations that make them feel as though they are part of a conforming herd. Apostates are also free—or, rather, "freethinkers." Having discarded religious faith, they feel free to read whatever they want, listen to whatever they want, think about whatever they want, discuss whatever they want, and let their minds wander or ponder as they will, without fear of eternally damaging their souls, angering their God, or disappointing their parents or pastor. Finally, apostates are life-lovers—or at least strong life-appreciators. They either don't believe in an afterlife, or they don't worry too much about it. Instead, they focus on the here and now, deriving joy, emotional sustenance, and individual purpose by engaging in this world and appreciating the time they have on earth.[15]

Of course, not all apostates exhibit all of the traits I've just broached. And my appraisal of what apostates are like—their personalities and qualities—is, of course, unavoidably subjective. More research is necessary to refute or support my impressions, to be sure.

PREDICTIONS

Will more people reject religion in the years ahead? Yes, I think so. In the next decade or two, rates of apostasy in America will likely increase. First off, the proportion of Americans disassociating themselves from religion has been swelling since the 1990s. For instance, in 2003, 10% of Americans did not believe in God, but that percentage doubled in a mere five years, so that in 2008, 20% of Americans did not believe in God—the highest rate of faithlessness in American history.[16] As these numbers continue to grow, we can expect apostasy to become more widely acceptable. And even though surveys currently reveal a general dislike of atheists among the American people, greater acceptance appears to be imminent, as evidenced by President Obama's inaugural speech, delivered on January 20, 2009, in front of nearly two million people, in which he described the United States as a nation of "Christians and Muslims, Jews and Hindus—and nonbelievers." This was the first time that an American president has ever acknowledged the existence of nonbelievers in such a public forum. Obama's inclusion of nonbelievers in his speech was not only a recognition of their increasing numbers but an indication of a growing acceptance of their presence in American society. This increase and acceptance of nonreligious Americans will make apostasy a much easier choice for those struggling with the decision of whether or not to reject their religion. It will make being an atheist or agnostic less of a stigmatized identity. Additionally, the mushrooming of atheist and secular humanist groups around the country will serve as a source of encouragement for people who lose their faith and seek a group of like-minded people for social support and intellectual pollination. I am also certain that the Internet will play a crucial role. In the past, if someone—especially someone living in a very religious part of the country—felt his or her faith evaporating, or an alienation from religion growing, he or she would usually have to navigate this potentially difficult process in relative isolation. But with the Internet, one can reach out to others in similar straits in a matter of seconds. An individual leaning toward apostasy can immediately connect with people who have rejected their religion from a variety of backgrounds and traditions, instantly connecting with legions of like-minded men and women who are reaching out to one another, sharing ideas, discussing, debating, and expressing themselves on countless websites devoted to spreading and supporting secularity.

I would not, however, go so far as to predict an imminent or irreversible wave of apostasy resulting in widespread secularization. A decline in religiosity is by no means inevitable. While the factors that might contribute to increased secularization are numerous, so too are those that could just as easily hinder secularization. For instance, if the potential ravages of global warming begin to manifest themselves with greater frequency, if the gap between rich and poor continues to grow, if more and more Americans lack decent jobs, adequate health care, good child and elder care, and if the economy tanks for significant stretches—in short, if life in the decades ahead becomes harder and more precarious for most Americans, then I am sure that apostasy will remain decidedly uncommon. After all, religion is one of the great sources of psychological comfort and social solidarity in times of widespread insecurity.

But enough prognostication. This book is not about the future. It is about apostasy in the here and now: contemporary men and women in the United States who once were religious but are no longer. They have shed their faith and religious involvement in favor of a more secular life. I have tried to capture their ideas, opinions, insights, experiences, and personal stories. I hope that the accounts and observations presented in this book have helped shed some light on their motivations and struggles, their losses and their gains.

APPENDIX

———∿———

Research Methods and Sample Characteristics

Although I have had numerous conversations with many apostates over the past two years—some brief, others extensive—the research for this book is specifically based on 87 formal interviews conducted between May 2008 and March 2010. By formal, I mean that these interviews were conducted in such a manner that the individuals knew that they were being interviewed for my book, they were informed of the research questions motivating the interview, and they consented to the process. A designated time was set aside to conduct each interview and a structured set of questions was referred to, although most interviews generally proceeded as open-ended conversations. Each interview lasted approximately one hour, although a few were closer to a half hour, and a few others were closer to two hours.

Of the 87 interviews, 49 were conducted by me, with the remaining 38 being conducted by my research assistants; most of my assistants conducted approximately two interviews each. These research assistants were part of a seminar I taught at Pitzer College in the spring of 2009, wherein they received extensive training on how to conduct these interviews. Nearly all 87 interviews were tape-recorded and later transcribed for analysis; a few were tape-recorded but could not be transcribed for various technical reasons; and two interviews were not tape-recorded, but extensive notes were taken throughout those interviews. Of the 87 interviews, 16 were conducted over the phone, and the remaining 71 were done in person, face to face.

Apostates were generally found via a nonpurposive, judgmental sampling method in which I sought out potential informants based on my knowledge of their status as someone who had once been religious. When individuals agreed to an interview, I proceeded to find more apostates by employing a standard snowball sampling method in which additional individuals were recommended to me by those already interviewed; after interviewing a small cluster of friends and acquaintances, I subsequently asked them if they could recommend others who might be suitable for my study. From those recommended interviewees, I asked for additional contacts, and thus my sample grew and grew. Of the 87 men and women interviewed for this study, 6 were friends (people whom I see or socialize with on a fairly regular basis), 19 were acquaintances (people I knew prior to the interview, such as former students or colleagues—but not individuals whom I regularly see or socialize with), and 62 were complete strangers (people whom I had no contact with before or after the interviews).

Although men and women from a variety of ages, backgrounds, races, ethnicities, religious traditions, occupations, and geographical locations participated in these interviews, mine was a convenience sample and hence nonrandom. Thus, valid statistical generalizability to the wider population of American apostates is not possible.

Of those who were interviewed, 47 were male and 40 were female; 6% were in their late teens, 30% were in their twenties, 23% were in their thirties, 16% were in their forties, 15% were in their fifties, 8% were in their sixties, and 3% were in their seventies. Approximately 48% of my informants were raised in California, with others being raised in the Midwest (10%), the East Coast (11%), the South (9%), the Southwest (3%), and the

Pacific Northwest (3%). About 10% of interviewees were from other countries, such as England, Saudi Arabia, Ghana, and the Philippines. The percentages of where people were raised are approximations because sometimes people were raised in more than one state or country. In terms of educational attainment, approximately 5% had only completed a high school education; approximately 30% had either completed some college or were currently enrolled in college; approximately 33% had completed a bachelor's degree; and approximately 30% had completed an advanced/graduate degree. As for racial/ethnic identification, approximately 64% of my sample self-identified as White or Caucasian; 12% as Latino/a, Chicano/a, Hispanic, or Mexican-American; 12% as mixed-race or "other"; 7% as Asian, Asian-American, or Pacific Islander; and 3% as Black or African-American (these are approximations because there were a few who classi-fied themselves in atypical ways, such as "Celtic," "Jewish," or "Persian"). Finally, in terms of the religious identity that they were raised in or once claimed but no longer identify with, approx-imately 50% had been some denomination of Protestant Christian, 27% had been Catholic, 7% had been Jewish, 5% had been Mormon, 5% had been Muslim, and the remainder were of mixed/combined religious backgrounds.

For further details on the demographics of my interviewees (such as political preferences, occupations, or class background based on occupation of parents), see the table below.

Date of Interview	Gender	Age	Where Raised	Occupation	Highest Ed	Race/ Ethnicity	Mother's Occ.	Father's Occ.	Pol. Party	Former/Ex-
1. 5/9/08	M	Mid-thirties	Southern CA	Library manager	Some college	White	Telephone operator	Transportation engineer	Libertarian	Pentecostal Christian
2. 5/14/08	F	Mid-thirties	upstate NY/ Southern CA	Fundraiser	BA	Black	Hospital administrator	CPA	Dem	Nondenominational Christian
3. 5/16/08	F	Late twenties	Southern CA	Assistant director of nonprofit	BA	White	Teacher's aide	Police officer/ truck driver	Dem	Lutheran
4. 5/18/08	M	Early thirties	Southern CA	Comm. college prof.	MA	Italian-American	Spiritual counselor	Nurse	Independent	Evangelical Christian
5. 5/27/08	F	Late twenties	Northern CA	Student/ tutor	AA	White	Dance teacher	Carpenter	Dem	Christian
6. 5/27/08	F	Mid-forties	Southern CA	Architect	MA	White	School teacher	Realtor	Nonpartisan	Pentecostal Christian
7. 6/2/08	M	Mid-forties	Southern CA	Audio-visual librarian	BA	White	Hairdresser	Contractor	Independent	Christian
8. 6/3/08	M	Early twenties	Southern CA	Student	Some college	White	Librarian	Think-tank consultant	Independent	Conservative Jewish
9. 6/6/08	M	Early twenties	Southern CA	Law student	BA	White	Spiritual counselor	Nurse	Green/ Independent	Evangelical Christian
10. 6/10/08	F	Late twenties	Southern CA	Adjunct professor	MA	White	Dental assistant	Teach specialist for electric co.	Green/Dem	Christian

No. / Date	Sex	Age	Location	Occupation	Education	Ethnicity	Occupation	Occupation	Party	Religion
11. 9/12/08	M	Early sixties	CO	Professor	PhD	Chicano/Latino	Homemaker/vegetable picker	Farmhand	Dem	Catholic
12. 9/29/08	F	Early twenties	Southern CA	Student	Some college	Mexican	Administrative assistant	Video editor	Dem	Catholic
13. 10/8/08	F	Mid-twenties	Southern CA	Grad students	MA	Caucasian, ¼ Native American	Oil analyst	Museum curator/gun shop owner	Republican/Libertarian	Seventh Day Adventist
14. 10/8/08	F	Late thirties	IL	Writer	BA	White	Homemaker/librarian	Christian youth director	Dem	Baptist/Presbyterian
15. 10/15/08	F	Late twenties	MO	Grad student	BA	"Other"	Speech pathologist	Food industry consultant	Not registered	Jewish
16. 10/19/08	M	Late fifties	Ghana	Computer programmer	Some college	Black	Homemaker	Farmer	Dem	Jehovah's Witness
17. 10/29/08	M	Mid-sixties	CO	Retired dentist	Doctorate in dentistry	White	Homemaker	Painter/contractor	Dem	Lutheran
18. 10/29/08	F	Early twenties	Southern CA	Receptionist/student	Some college	White	Secretary	Construction superintendent	Dem	Mormon
19. 11/4/08	M	Late thirties	TX	College instructor	PhD	White	Nurse	Accountant	Not registered	Christian
20. 11/18/08	M	Early thirties	Belgium	Actor	AA	White	Teacher	Farmer	N/A	Catholic
21. 11/11/08	M	Late twenties	GA	Bartender/writer	BS	White	Teacher/office clerk	Accountant	Dem	Catholic
22. 11/14/08	M	Mid-twenties	MI	Student	BA	White	Teacher	Salesman	Green	Lutheran

(continued)

CONTINUED

Date of Interview	Gender	Age	Where Raised	Occupation	Highest Ed	Race/Ethnicity	Mother's Occ.	Father's Occ.	Pol. Party	Former/Ex-
23. 11/15/08	F	Late twenties	NY/KS	Martial arts instructor/ actress	BA	White	Special needs instructor	Portfolio manager	Dem	Jewish
24. 11/16/08	M	Mid-fifties	VA	Flower breeder	Some college	White	Librarian	Professor	Dem	Evangelical Christian
25. 11/23/08	M	Early fifties	CO	Scientist at drug company	BA	White	Homemaker/ greenhouse worker	Truck driver	Dem	Christian
26. 11/23/08	M	Mid-thirties	Southern CA	Health consultant/ writer/teacher	MA	White	Homemaker	Gasman	Dem	Mormon
27. 11/26/08	M	Late thirties	IL	College advisor	BA	White	Homemaker/ nursery school teacher	Social worker	Not registered	Christian
28. 12/1/08	M	Early thirties	OH	Thesaurus editor	BA	White	Homemaker	Musician/ railroad engineer	Not registered	United Methodist
29. 12/2/08	F	Early twenties	Southern CA	Student	Some college	Mexican	Book-keeper	Unemployed	Dem	Christian
30. 12/7/08	M	Early sixties	ID	High school teacher/ musician	BA, plus teaching credential	White	Nurse	Carpenter	Republican	Mormon
31. 12/18/08	M	Late forties	Southern CA	Elementary school teacher	MA	White	Teacher	Homemaker	Green	Evangelical/Baptist/ Mennonite/Catholic

32. 1/21/09	F	Late twenties	Southern CA	Nonprofit program coordinator	BA	White	Nurse	Forklift driver	Green	Nondenominational Christian
33. 1/23/09	M	Late forties	Southern CA	Small business owner	BA	White	Homemaker	Budget analyst/defense contractor	Dem	Catholic
34. 1/26/09	F	Early twenties	Southern CA	Bank teller	High school	White/Native American	Phone operator/housewife	Sheet metal worker/small business owner	Independent	Christian
35. 2/4/09	F	Mid-thirties	MN	Law student	BA	White	Computer programmer/homemaker	Meat cutter	Dem	Jehovah's Witness
36. 2/9/09	M	Early seventies	MD/GA	Retired schoolteacher	MA	White	Homemaker/secretary	Federal employee	Dem	Methodist
37. 2/18/09	F	Early thirties	Southern CA	Waitress	Some college	White	Secretary/office clerk	Landscaper	Dem	Christian
38. 2/25/09	F	Mid-fifties	PA	Professor	PhD	White	Homemaker/office clerk	Machine operator	**	Christian
39. 2/25/09	M	Late forties	NY	Writer	BFA	White	Nurse	Lawyer	Independent/Dem	Catholic
40. 3/3/09	F	Mid-twenties	Northern CA	Food server/student	Some college	White	Unemployed	Truck driver	**	Christian
41. 3/4/09	F	Late thirties	Canada/CA	Sales account manager	BA	White	Homemaker	Doctor	Dem	Catholic
42. 3/5/09	M	Late teens	Northern CA	Lifeguard/student	Some college	White	Prosecutor	Professor	None	Christian

(continued)

CONTINUED

Date of Interview	Gender	Age	Where Raised	Occupation	Highest Ed	Race/Ethnicity	Mother's Occ.	Father's Occ.	Pol. Party	Former/Ex-
43. 3/6/09	M	Late fifties	Southern CA	Small business owner	MA	Portuguese	Homemaker	Self-employed	Dem	Catholic
44. 3/6/09	F	Mid-fifties	GA	Doctor	Med school	Jewish	Homemaker	Shoe salesman	Dem	Orthodox Jewish
45. 3/8/09	M	Late teens	OH	Student	Some college	White	Homemaker/artist	CEO of investment firm	None	Christian
46. 3/8/09	F	Mid-sixties	NY	Retired apartment manager	High school	White	Cook	Carpenter	**	Baptist
47. 3/9/08	F	Early forties	Philippines	Director of Research	MA	Filipino	Owner/director of private school	Sugar salesman	Dem	Catholic/Christian
48. 3/9/09	M	Mid-fifties	Northern CA	Student	Some college	White	Unknown	Iron worker	Dem	Christian
49. 3/12/09	F	Early twenties	Southern CA	Student	Some college	White	Librarian/admissions officer	Elementary school teacher	None	Nondenominational Christian
50. 3/14/09	M	Mid-twenties	Northern CA	Grad school student	BA	Indian	Teacher	CEO of tech corp.	None	Hindu
51. 3/17/09	F	Late thirties	Southern CA	Homemaker	BA	Chicana	Unclear	Factory worker	Green/Dem	Catholic
52. 3/18/09	F	Early fifties	Southern CA/Guam	Spiritual advisor	High school	Pacific Islander	Warehouse worker	Auto mechanic	**	Southern Baptist
53. 3/19/09	F	Late sixties	England	Retired editor	BA	White	Homemaker	Engineer	Dem	Catholic

No. / Date	Gender	Age	Origin	Occupation	Education	Race/Ethnicity			Party	Religion
54. 3/19/09	F	Early fifties	England	Librarian	MA	White	High school teacher	Manager of shipping company	Dem	Christian
55. 3/20/09	M	Late fifties	CT	Attorney	PhD	White	Homemaker/ school teacher	Professor	Dem	Congregationalist
56. 3/20/09	F	Late teens	NY	Student	Some college	Thai-American	Homemaker	Owner of landscape company	Dem	Jewish
57. 3/23/09	M	Mid-twenties	TX	Student	Some college	White	Teacher	Engineer	Republican	Catholic
58. 3/23/09	F	Late teens	Southern CA	Student	Some college	White	Homemaker	Expert witness for insurance co.	Dem	Catholic
59. 3/24/09	M	Early twenties	Southern CA	Student	Some college	Latino/ Chicano	Café manager	Groundskeeper	Dem	Catholic
60. 3/25/09	M	Late thirties	NY	Professor	PhD	African American	Junior high teacher	Musician/mass transit authority employee	Not registered	Pentecostal Christian
61. 3/26/09	M	Late seventies	Southern CA	**	AA	Chicano	Homemaker	Laborer	Dem	Catholic
62. 3/26/09	F	Late forties	Germany/ Belgium/ Spain	Professor	PhD	White	Translator	Chemist	Dem	Catholic
63. 3/26/09	M	Mid-forties	Southern CA	In-home health care provider	Some college	Chicano	**	**	Socialist	Jehovah's Witness

(continued)

CONTINUED

Date of Interview	Gender	Age	Where Raised	Occupation	Highest Ed	Race/Ethnicity	Mother's Occ.	Father's Occ.	Pol. Party	Former/Ex-
64. 4/3/09	M	Mid-thirties	Saudi Arabia	Small business owner	BA	White	Principal	Civil engineer	Dem	Muslim
65. 4/7/09	M	Mid-twenties	Southern CA	Elementary schoolteacher	MA	Mexican-Italian-American	Homemaker/babysitter	High school teacher/job counselor	Dem	Catholic
66. 4/11/09	M	Mid-forties	Southern CA	Sales	Some college	Mexican American	Receptionist	Pressman	Dem	Catholic
67. 4/14/09	M	Early sixties	IL	Student	BA	Celtic	School teacher	Machinist	None	Catholic
68. 4/15/09	F	Late thirties	Southern CA	Homemaker	BA	White	Grocery checker	Computer programmer	Dem	Mormon
69. 4/17/09	M	Mid-thirties	NJ	Student/carpenter	Some college	White	Psychologist	Electrical engineer	Independent	Christian
70. 4/17/09	F	Late teens	OR	Student	Some college	Lebanese/Arab-American	Homemaker	Small business owner	Dem	Muslim
71. 4/17/09	M	Late twenties	TX	Law student	BA	Persian	**	**	**	Muslim
72. 4/19/09	F	Mid-forties	Southern CA	Marriage counselor	MA	White	Homemaker	Produce business owner	Independent	Christian
73. 4/23/09	M	Mid-twenties	Southern CA	Student	Some college	Filipino	Teacher	Musician/artist	None	Catholic
74. 4/24/09	F	Late forties	Mexico	Professor	PhD	Mexican	Homemaker	Engineer	Dem	Catholic
75. 4/24/09	M	Early fifties	Southern CA	Psychologist	MA	White	Interior designer	Engineer	Dem	Catholic
76. 4/25/09	F	Early fifties	NY	Social Worker	MA	White	**	**	**	Christian

No. / Date	Sex	Age	Location	Occupation	Education	Race/ethnicity			Party	Religion
77. 4/25/09	M	Early thirties	NY	Writer	BA	White	Psycho-dramatist	President of company	Dem	Jewish
78. 4/26/09	F	Mid-seventies	Southern CA	**	High school	Mexican American	Worked at restaurant	County employee/flood control	Dem	Catholic/Presbyterian
79. 5/3/09	F	Mid-fifties	WI	Math teacher	BA	White	Fashion designer	Attorney	Dem	Melchite/Roman Catholic
80. 6/4/09	M	Mid-forties	MD	Adjunct professor	PhD	White	School teacher	School teacher	Dem	Catholic
81. 11/18/09	M	Early sixties	Southern CA	Substitute teacher	BA	White	Homemaker	Contractor/carpenter	Dem/Green	Presbyterian
82. 11/30/09	M	Early forties	Southern CA	Video game artist	High school	Irish-Italian	Hairdresser/retail clerk	Plumber/salesman	Dem	Catholic/Christian
83. 12/7/09	M	Mid-thirties	ND	Writer/film maker	MBA	White	Insurance claim adjuster	Accountant	Independent	Lutheran
84. 12/10/09	F	Mid-twenties	WA	Student	BA	White	Homemaker	Marine	Progressive	Christian
85. 12/15/09	M	Mid-twenties	Southern CA	Student	Some college	Mexican/Hispanic	Teacher's assistant	Truck driver	Independent	Catholic
86. 1/8/10	F	Mid-twenties	Bangladesh	Grad student	MA	Bengali	Homemaker/manager of bakery	Economic policy advisor	**	Muslim
87. 3/18/1-	F	Early forties	CA	Homemaker	BA	Hispanic/Basque	**	Rancher/farmer	**	Catholic

** Answers were unclear, inaudible, unknown, or inapplicable.
Race/ethnicity: self-determined/stated by individual being interviewed.

NOTES

INTRODUCTION
1. Kosmin and Keysar (2008), p. 7. And while this book deals mostly with apostasy and increased secularity in the United States, there are also signs of increased apostasy and secularity in Canada as well (Altemeyer, 2010; Fitzpatrick, 2010). For example, Reginald Bibby (2002) reports that, concerning belief in God specifically, back in 1985 61% of Canadians said that they "definitely do," but that dropped to 49% in 2000.
2. For data on the increase of secularity, see Kosmin and Keysar (2008); Pew Forum U.S. Religious Landscape Survey: http://religions.pewforum.org/affiliations; Harris Polls: http://www.harris-interactive.com/harris_poll/index.asp?PID=707 and also http://www.harrisinteractive.com/harris_poll/index.asp?PID=982; *Parade* "Spirituality Poll results" survey: http://www.parade.com/news/2009/10/04-spirituality-poll-results.html from October 4, 2009.
3. For information about the growth of secular groups, see *New York Times*: http://www.nytimes.com/2009/04/27/us/27atheist.html; growth of FFRF: Freedom from Religion Foundation: http://www.ffrf.org/membership/reports/2006.php. For the growth of secular student groups, see Gorski (2009) and also Secular Student Alliance: http://www.secularstudents.org/; for the growth of secularity among youth, see Putnam study: http://abcnews.go.com/Politics/story?id=7513343&page=1; see also Landsberg (2010).
4. Hunsberger and Altemeyer (2006), p. 15. See also Gottlieb (2008); Bainbridge (2005); Kosmin and Keysar (2006); and Tamney et al. (1989).
5. For definitions of apostasy, see Beit-Hallahmi (2007), p. 302; Bromley (1988), p. 12; and Caplovitz and Sherrow (1977), pp. 30–31.
6. See Mauss (1969) and Brinkerhoff and Burke (1980).

7. For further discussion of this process, see Perry et al. (1980); Roozen (1980); Hadaway (1989); Leavy (1988); Pasquale (2010); Hefland (2009); and Smith (2010).
8. Albrecht et al. (1988), p. 62.
9. Walter and Davie (1998); Miller and Hoffman (1995); Miller and Stark (2002); Beit-Hallahmi and Argyle (1997); Beit-Hallahmi (2005); Batson et al. (1993); Rice (2003); Hayes (2000); Veevers and Cousineau (1980); and Sullins (2006).
10. For an extensive literature review comparing and contrasting the political values of secular people and religious people, see Zuckerman (2009a).
11. Berger (1963), p. 35.
12. Baker (2008); Sherkat (2003); Sherkat (2008); and Johnson (1997). See also the recent Harris Poll that found that 86% of Americans without a college education believe in the resurrection of Jesus Christ, but only 64% of Americans with a postgraduate degree believe so. See http://www.harrisinteractive.com/harris_poll/index.asp? PID=359.
13. Hadaway (1989), p. 214.
14. For a detailed description of my sample, see the appendix.
15. Johnson (1998), p.118. See also Paulhus (1984).

CHAPTER 1
1. *American Exorcism: Expelling Demons in the Land of Plenty*, by Michael Cuneo (2001).
2. Harris Interactive Poll 2008: http://www.harrisinteractive.com/harris_poll/index.asp?PID=982; see also the Baylor Religion Survey: http://www.thearda.com/quickstats/qsdir.asp.
3. Check out this website for more info: http://www.blasphemychallenge.com/.
4. Comte-Sponville (2006), pp. 5–6.

CHAPTER 2
1. For recently published accounts of people who emphasize that their apostasy was triggered by an inability to believe in the manifestly unbelievable, see Babinski (1995); Warraq (2003); Southerton (2004); Loftus (2008); and Smith (2010).
2. Bible passages: Exodus 12:29, Hosea 10:14, II Kings 2:23, 24; Numbers 31:1–18, Deuteronomy 2:33–35. Qu'ran passages: Sura II:191, Sura XIV:16–17, Sura V:38, Sura XXII:19–22, Sura XXIII:6, and also Warraq (2003). Mormon passages: II Nephi 5:21, II Nephi 25:9 and also Doctrines and Covenants 132:41–63.

3. Ranke-Heinemann (1992), p. 60.
4. Craig (2007), p. 74. For surveys indicating Americans' dislike of atheists, see Edgell et al. (2006). For a refutation of the notion that atheists are immoral, see Beit-Hallahmi (2010).

CHAPTER 3
1. Gallup and Lindsay (1999), pp. 45–46, and http://religions.pew-forum.org/maps.

CHAPTER 4
1. A 2009 Pew Forum survey found that while only 24% of Protestants in America support gay marriage, and 39% of Catholics support gay marriage, a full 67% of religious unaffil-iated Americans do, indicating a strong correlation between supporting gay marriage and being nonreligious. For details, see http://pewforum.org/Gay-Marriage-and-Homosexuality/Public-Opinion-on-Gay-Marriage-Opponents-Consistently-Outnumber-Supporters.aspx.
2. See Heiner (1992) for a discussion of irreligion and deviance.
3. As Altemeyer and Hunsberger (1997) have argued, the apostates they studied "had often paid a heavy price for their apostasy: alienation from their families and loss of friends" (p. 215).
4. See Wolkomir (2006); Dolan (2010); Schnoor (2006); Linneman and Clendenen (2010); and Sherkat (2002).

CHAPTER 5
1. This conversation/interview was not recorded; hence, I have quoted Frank, rather than put his words into italics, which is reserved only for extended recorded statements.
2. Regnerus (2007), p. 214. See also Adamczyk (2009).
3. For more information about and research on abstinence pledge movements, see Bearman and Bruckner (2001).
4. As Lauren Winner (2005) notes, many religious women who remain virgins until marriage often grapple for years with emo-tional trouble based on such extensive religiously inspired sexual denial. See also Purcell (1985).
5. Schlessinger (1998). See also Manning and Zuckerman (2005) and Parrinder (1996).
6. For a summation of the studies which discuss the sexual behav-iors and attitudes of secular people in comparison with religious people, see also Manning and Zuckerman (2005) and Zuckerman (2009a).

7. See "Patient Teenagers? A Comparison of the Sexual Behavior of Virginity Pledgers and Matched Nonpledgers," http://pediatrics. aappublications.org/cgi/content/abstract/123/1/e110.
8. Regnerus (2007), p. 73.
9. Regnerus (2007), pp. 66–67, 81.
10. See Regnerus (2007), p. 137, and also Bearman and Bruckner (2001) and Barkan (2006).
11. For research on the correlation between religiosity, secularity, and STD rates, and so forth, see Paul (2009); Zuckerman (2009a); Blumenthal (2009); and Talbot (2008).

CHAPTER 6

1. William Lobdell's story is recounted in *Losing My Religion: How I Lost My Faith Reporting on Religion in America—and Found Unexpected Peace.*
2. Lobdell (2009), p. 142.
3. Lobdell (2009), p. 244.
4. Everett (2008).
5. Everett (2008), pp. 270–271.
6. For data on low levels of theism in Estonia, see Eurobarometer, 2005, #225, "Social Values, Science, and Technology," http://ec. europa.eu/public_opinion/archives/eb_special_en.htm.
7. See Stark and Finke (2000) p. 23; Beit-Hallahmi (2007); Gross and Simmons (2009); and Wuthnow (1989). Secularity is highest among social scientists—particularly anthropologists—because such scholars are deeply familiar with, and ever cognizant of, the degree to which our values, beliefs, and worldviews are strongly shaped by how, when, and where we are raised.
8. Argyle (2000), p. 25.
9. Berger (1967).
10. Bruce (1996), p. 49.
11. Berger (1967).
12. Kosmin (2009).

CHAPTER 7

1. Keysar (2007). For additional research on gender differences and religion, see Miller and Hoffman (1995); Bellamy et al. (2002); Stark (2002); Beit-Hallahmi and Argyle (1997); Altemeyer and Hunsberger (1997, chap. 7); Veevers and Cousineau (1980); Hunt (2005, chap. 5); and Beit-Hallahmi (2005).
2. Scott and Leonhardt (2005). For additional research on class and religiosity, see Baker (2008); Davidson (1977); Stark (1972);

Demerath (1965); Kosmin and Lachman (1993); and Norris and Inglehart (2004, pp. 108–110).

3. For studies that show a correlation between increased educational attainment and decreased religious belief, see Sherkat (2003); Johnson (1997); Gallup and Castelli (1989); Hadaway and Roof (1988); Roof and McKinney (1987); Wilson and Sherkat (1994); and Wuthnow and Mellinger (1978).

4. Although it is beyond my own expertise, a small but growing body of research is correlating atheism with innate intelligence. See, for example, Kanazawa (2010); Lynn et al. (2009); and Nyborg (2008). See also Darren Sherkat (2006, 2009), who has found that secular people score markedly higher on verbal ability tests than religious people do (irrespective of educational attainment). He has also found that people who view the Bible as a book of fables have substantially higher levels of verbal sophistication than people who view the Bible as the actual word of God and that secular people score markedly higher than religious people on indicators of scientific proficiency than religious people have.

CHAPTER 8

1. Warren (2002), pp. 37–38.
2. Beit-Hallahmi (2007), p. 306.
3. Beit-Hallahmi (2010) and Zuckerman (2009a).
4. Bengston (2010), p. 17.
5. Golumbaski (1997).
6. Jensen (2006); Paul (2005); Fajnzylber et al. (2002); Fox and Levin (2000); and Zuckerman (2009a).
7. Zuckerman (2009a) and Ellison et al. (2003).
8. For a summation/discussion of numerous studies attesting to these matters, see Zuckerman (2009a).
9. Kohlberg (1973). See also Smith (2010).
10. Beit-Hallahmi (2007, 2010); Zuckerman (2008); and Nielsen (1990).
11. Lewis (1952), p. 227.
12. See also Pasquale (2010), who found in his study of secular group affiliates that the vast majority of atheists and agnostics most commonly found meaning in life from family, helping others, nature, friends, children, love, art, and so forth.
13. Zuckerman (2008, 2009b).
14. Regnerus (2007), p. 43.
15. Epstein (2009), p. xiv.
16. Argyle (2000), chap. 10; Nooney and Woodrum (2002).

17. Jesse Smith (2010), in his interviews with atheists who had been formerly religious, also found that "liberation" was a common feeling among his interviewees.
18. Harper (2007).
19. Edgell et al. (2006).
20. http://people-press.org/report/?pageid=386.
21. Newport (1999) and Hunter (1990).
22. Crossan (2010), p. 70.
23. Caputo (2001), pp. 2–3.
24. Duin (2008).

CHAPTER 9

1. Nelsen (1990). See also Bengston (2010).
2. For studies illustrating the degree that parental religious beliefs will determine the religiosity of children, see Smith and Denton (2005); Sherkat (2003); Bibby (2002); McGuire (2002); Stark and Finke (2000); Argyle (2000); Sherkat (1998); Hood, Spilka, Hunsberger, and Gorsuch (1996); Sherkat and Wilson (1995); Willits and Crider (1989); Kleugel (1980); Acock and Bengston (1978); and Manning (2010). For studies indicating parental influence on apostasy, see Hunsberger and Brown (1984); Barrow (1972); Sandomirsky and Wilson (1990); and Sherkat (1991b).
3. For further elaboration, see Bader and Desmond (2006) and King and Mueller (2004).
4. Virtually nothing has been written about how secular parents raise their children. The only exceptions I am aware of are the pioneering works of Christel Manning (2010) and Vern L. Bengston (2010).
5. Nall (2010).
6. Altemeyer (2010), p. 4.

CHAPTER 10

1. See also Smith (2010). For a clear articulation of how apostasy can entail a gradual process taking several years, see Chapter 2 from *Godless*, by Dan Barker (2008).
2. Campbell (1971), p. 36.
3. Hunt (2005), p. 64.
4. See Bader and Desmond (2006); Hayes and Pittelkow (1993); Ecklund and Scheitle (2007); Ozorak (1989); Albrecht, Cornwall, and Cunningham (1988); Hunsberger (1983); King, Furrow, and Roth (2002); Myers (1996a, 1996b); Acock (1984); Erickson (1992); Cornwall (1998); and Nelsen (1990).

5. Sherkat (2003); Lawton and Bures (2001); Beit-Hallahmi and Argyle (1997); Hunsberger (1985); Johnson, (1997); Zuckerman (2009a); and Baker (2008).
6. For a more theoretical discussion of this process, see Peter Berger (1967).
7. See Hout (2003) and Stark and Finke (2000).
8. See Kosmin (2008); Keysar (2007); Greeley and Hout (2006); Grupp and Newman (1973); Nassi (1981); Zuckerman (2009a); Hoffman and Miller (1997); Smidt (2005); Guth et al. (2005); Beit-Hallahmi (2007); and Grasmick et al. (1992).
9. Hout and Fischer (2002).
10. Weber (1991), pp. 236–237; Osborne (1993); and Manning and Zuckerman (2005).
11. Moore et al. (1998).
12. This phenomenon is astutely and insightfully illustrated in the wonderful, sociologically rich book Souls and Bodies, by David Lodge (1980).
13. Rose (2005). See also Regnerus (2007), p. 96.
14. Linneman and Clendenen (2010).
15. Sura XVI:106—quoted in Warraq (2003), p. 17.
16. Revelation 21:8.
17. 2 Nephi 28:21–23.
18. DeLamater and Myers (2011).
19. Smith (2007).
20. See Regnerus (2007); Hardy and Raffaelli (2003); and Meier (2003).
21. Wilcox (2002).
22. See Yip (1997, 2002).
23. See also Linneman and Clendenen (2010).
24. See Lee and Bullivant (2010).

CONCLUSION

1. See Pinker (2002), p. 63.
2. Wrong (1961).
3. Campbell (1971), p. 29.
4. For evidence of secularization, see Haught (2010); Bruce (2002); Brown (2001); and Shand (1998).
5. Froese (2008), pp. 2, 20–21.
6. Bibby (2002), pp. 58–60. Others who suggest that religious belief is an essential component to the human condition include Hamer (2004), p. 6; Greeley (1972), pp. 1, 16; Barrett (2004), p. 108.
7. Altemeyer and Hunsberger (1997).

8. Hecht (2003); Thrower (1979).
9. For further discussion, see Campbell (1971), chap. 5.
10. See also Pasquale (2010).
11. Paulos (2008).
12. For further elaboration, see Altemeyer (2010), pp. 6–7.
13. As Ibn Warraq has commented about apostates from Islam: "What is most striking is their fearlessness, their moral courage, and their moral commitment to telling the truth. They all face social ostracism, the loss of friends and family, a deep inner spiritual anguish and loneliness—and occasionally the death penalty if discovered" (2003), p. 135.
14. See Altemeyer and Hunsberger (1997); Kanazawa (2010); Hayes (2000); McAllister (1998); and Sherkat (2006, 2009).
15. See Kurtz (1994); Aronson (2008); and Maisel (2009).
16. Harris Interactive Poll, January 21–27, 2003, and November 10–17, 2008.

REFERENCES

Acock, Alan. 1984. "Parents and Their Children: The Study of Inter-Generation Influence." *Sociology and Social Research* 68: 151–171.

Acock, Alan, and Vern Bengston. 1978. "On the Relative Influence of Mothers and Fathers: A Covariance Analysis of Political and Religious Socialization." *Journal of Marriage and the Family* 40: 519–530.

Adamczyk, Amy. 2009. "Socialization and Selection in the Link between Friends' Religiosity and the Transition to Sexual Intercourse." *Sociology of Religion* 70(1): 5–27.

Adler, Patricia, and Peter Adler. 1997. *Constructions of Deviance: Social Power, Context, and Interaction*. Belmont, CA: Wadsworth.

Albrecht, S.L., Cornwall, Marie, and Perry Cunningham. 1988. "Religious Leave-Taking: Disengagement and Disaffiliation among Mormons," in *Falling from the Faith: Causes and Consequences of Religious Apostasy*, edited by David Bromley, pp. 62–80. Newbury Park, CA: Sage.

Ali, Ayaan Hirsi. 2007. *Infidel*. New York: Free Press.

Altemeyer, Bob. 2010. "Atheism and Secularity in North America," in *Atheism and Secularity, Volume II*, edited by Phil Zuckerman. Santa Barbara, CA: Preager ABC-CLIO.

Altemeyer, Bob, and Bruce Hunsberger. 1997. *Amazing Conversions: Why Some Turn to Faith and Others Abandon Religion*. Amherst, NY: Prometheus.

Argyle, Michael. 2000. *Psychology and Religion: An Introduction*. London: Routledge.

Aronson, Ronald. 2008. *Living without God: New Directions for Atheists, Agnostics, Secularists, and the Undecided*. Berkeley, CA: Counterpoint.

Babinski, Edward. 1995. *Leaving the Fold: Testimonies of Former Fundamentalists*. Amherst, NY: Prometheus.

Bader, Christopher, and Scott Desmond. 2006. "Do as I Say and as I Do: The Effects of Consistent Parental Beliefs and Behaviors Upon Religious Transmission." *Sociology of Religion* 67: 313–329.

Bainbridge, William Sims. 2005. "Atheism." *Interdisciplinary Journal of Research on Religion* 1 (2): 1–25.

Baker, Joseph. 2008. "An Investigation of the Sociological Patterns of Prayer Frequency and Content." *Sociology of Religion* 69: 169–185.

Barkan, Steven. 2006. "Religiosity and Premarital Sex in Adulthood." *Journal for the Scientific Study of Religion* 45(3): 407–417.

Barker, Dan. 2008. *Godless: How an Evangelical Preacher Became One of America's Leading Atheists*. Berkeley, CA: Ulysses Press.

Barrett, Justin. 2004. *Why Would Anyone Believe in God?* Walnut Creek, CA: AltaMira.

Barrow, M. L. 1972. *The Blending American: Patterns of Intermarriage*. Chicago: Quadrangle Books.

Batson, C. D., Schoenrade, P., and Ventis, W. L. 1993. *Religion and the Individual: A Social-Psychological Perspective*. New York: Oxford University Press.

Bearman, Peter, and Hannah Bruckner. 2001. "Promising the Future: Virginity Pledges and First Intercourse." *American Journal of Sociology* 106: 859–912.

Becker, Gary. 1981. *A Treatise on the Family*. Cambridge, MA: Harvard University Press.

Becker, Howard. 1963. *Outsiders: Studies in the Sociology of Deviance*. New York: Free Press.

Beit-Hallahmi, Benjamin. 2010. "Morality and Immorality among the Irreligious," in *Atheism and Secularity, Volume I*, edited by Phil Zuckerman. Santa Barbara, CA: Praeger ABC-CLIO.

Beit-Hallahmi, Benjamin. 2007. "Atheists: A Psychological Profile," in *The Cambridge Companion to Atheism*, edited by Michael Martin, pp. 300–317. New York: Cambridge University Press.

Beit-Hallahmi, Benjamin. 2005. "Women, Psychological Feminity, and Religion," in *Handbook of the Psychology of Religion*, edited by D.M. Wulff. New York: Oxford University Press.

Beit-Hallahmi, Benjamin, and Michael Argyle. 1997. *The Psychology of Religious Behaviour, Belief, and Experience*. London: Routledge.

Bellah, Robert. 1970. *Beyond Belief*. New York: Harper and Row.

Bellamy, John, Alan Black, Keith Castle, Philip Hughes, and Peter Kaldor. 2002. *Why People Stop Going to Church*. Adelaide: Openbook.

Bengston, Vern. 2010. "The Non-religious and Family Transmission: Atheists, Agnostics, and 'None's'." Unpublished manuscript.

Berger, Peter. 1967. *The Sacred Canopy: Elements of a Sociological Theory of Religion*. Garden City, NY: Doubleday.

Berger, Peter. 1963. *Invitation to Sociology: A Humanist Perspective*. New York: Anchor Books.

Berger, Peter, Grace Davie, andf Effie Fokas. 2008. *Religious America, Secular Europe?* Burlington, VT: Ashgate.

Berkowitz, Peter. 2007. "The New New Atheism." *Wall Street Journal*, July 16. http://www.opinionjournal.com/editorial/feature.html?id=110010341.

Bibby, Reginald. 2002. *Restless Gods*. Toronto, CA: Stoddart.

Blumenthal, Max. 2009. "Will Palin Make It a Roguer GOP." *Los Angeles Times*, November 15, p. A36.

Brasher, Brenda. 1998. *Godly Women: Fundamentalism and Female Power*. New Brunswick, NJ: Rutgers University Press.

Bringhurst, Newell. 1981. *Saints, Slaves, and Blacks: The Changing Place of Black People within Mormonism*.Westport, CT: Greenwood.

Brinkerhoff, Merline, and Kathryn Burke. 1980. "Some Notes on 'Falling From Faith.' " 1980. *Sociological Analysis* 41(1): 41–54.

Brinkerhoff, Merlin, and Marlene Mackie. 1993. "Casting Off the Bonds of Organized Religion: A Religious-Careers Approach to the Study of Apostasy." *Review of Religious Research* 34(3): 235–257.

Bromley, David. 1998. *The Politics of Religious Apostasy*. Westport, CT: Praeger.

Bromley, David, ed. 1988. *Falling from the Faith: Causes and Consequences of Religious Apostasy*, Beverly Hills, CA: Sage.

Bromley, David. 1988. "Religious Disaffiliation: A Neglected Social Process," in *Falling from the Faith: Causes and Consequences of Religious Apostasy*, edited by David Bromley, 1–14. Beverly Hills, CA: Sage.

Brown, Callum. 2001. *The Death of Christian Britain*. London: Routledge.

Bruce, Steve. 2002. *God Is Dead: Secularization in the West*. Oxford: Blackwell.

Bruce, Steve. 2001. "Christianity in Britain, R.I.P." *Sociology of Religion* 62(2): 191–203.

Bruce, Steve. 1996. *Religion in the Modern World: From Cathedrals to Cults*. Oxford: Oxford University Press.

Bruce, Steve, ed. 1992. *Religion and Modernity: Sociologists and Historians Debate the Secularization Thesis*. New York: Oxford University Press.

Campbell, Colin. 1971. *Toward a Sociology of Irreligion*. New York: Herder and Herder.

Caplovitz, David, and Fred Sherrow. 1977. *The Religious Drop-Outs: Apostasy among College Graduates*. Beverly Hills, CA: Sage.

Caputo, John. 2001. *On Religion*. New York: Routledge.

Carrier, Richard. 2005. *Sense and Goodness without God: A Defense of Metaphysical Naturalism*. Bloomington, IN: AuthorHouse.

Charon, Joel, and Lee Garth Vigilant. 2009. *The Meaning of Sociology*. Upper Saddle River, NJ: Pearson-Prentice Hall.

Chaves, Mark. 1994. "Secularization as Declining Religious Authority." *Social Forces* 72: 749–774.

Chaves, Mark, and Laura Stephens. 2003. "Church Attendance in the United States," in *Handbook of the Sociology of Religion*, edited by Michele Dillon. New York: Cambridge University Press.

Chodorow, Nancy. 1978. *The Reproduction of Mothering: Psychoanalysis and the Sociology of Gender*. Berkeley: University of California Press.

Christiano, Kevin, William Swatos, and Peter Kivisto. 2002. *Sociology of Religion: Contemporary Developments*. Walnut Creek, CA: AltaMira.

Comte-Sponville, Andre. 2006. *The Little Book of Atheist Spirituality*. New York: Viking/Penguin.

Conley, Dalton. 2011. *You May Ask Yourself*. New York: W. W. Norton.

Cornwall, Marie. 1998. "The Determinants of Religious Behavior: A Theoretical Model and Empirical Test." *Social Forces* 68: 572–592.

Craig, William Lane. 2007, "Theistic Critiques of Athiesm," in *The Cambridge Companion to Atheism*, edited by Michael Martin. New York: Cambridge University Press.

Crockett, Alasdair, and David Voas. 2006. "Generations of Decline: Religious Change in 20th-Century Britain." *Journal for the Scientific Study of Religion* 45(5): 567–584.

Crooks, Robert, and Karla Baur. 1996. *Our Sexuality*. Albany, NY: Brooks/Cole.

Crossan, John Dominic. 2010. "Interview," in *Open Questions: Diverse Thinkers Discuss God, Religion, and Faith*, edited by Luis Rodrigues, pp. 55–73. Santa Barbara, CA: Praeger.

Cuneo, Michael. 2001. *American Exorcism: Expelling Demons in the Land of Plenty*. New York: Doubleday.

Cuzzort, R. P., and E. W. King, 1989. *Twentieth Century Social Thought*. Fort Worth, TX: Holt, Reinhart, and Winston.

Davidson, James D. 1977. "Socio-Economic Status and Ten Dimensions of Religious Commitment." *Sociology and Social Research* 61: 462–485.

Davie, Grace. 1999. "Europe: The Exception That Proves the Rule?" in *The Desecularization of the World*, edited by Peter Berger. Grand Rapids, MI: Eerdmans.

Dawkins, Richard. 2006. *The God Delusion*. Boston: Houghton Mifflin.

DeLamater, John, and Daniel Myers. 2011. *Social Psychology*. Belmont, CA: Wadsworth.

Demerath, N. J. III. 2007. "Secularization and Sacralization Deconstructed and Reconstructed," in *The SAGE Handbook of the Sociology of Religion*, edited by James Beckford and N. J. Demerath. Thousand Oaks, CA: Sage.

Demerath, N. J .III. 1965. *Social Class in American Protestantism*. Chicago: Rand-McNally.

Diaz-Stevens, Ana Maria. 1994. "Latinas and the Church," in *Hispanic Catholic Culture in the U.S.: Issues and Concerns*, edited by J. P. Dolan and A.F. Deck. Notre Dame, IN: University of Notre Dame Press.

Dobbelaere, Karel. 1981. *Secularization: A Mutli-Dimensional Concept*. London: Sage.

Dolan, Marua. 2010. "Effects of Bias on Gays Are Described." *Los Angeles Times*, January 15, p. A13.

Du Bois, W. E. B. 2003. *The Negro Church*. Walnut Creek, CA: AltaMira.

Dudley, Roger Louis. 1978. "Alienation from Religion in Adolescents from Fundamentalist Homes." *Journal for the Scientific Study of Religion* 17(4): 389–398.

Duin, Julia. 2008. "Half of Americans Believe in Angels," *Washington Post*, September 19, http://www.washingtontimes.com/news/2008/sep/19/half-of-americans-believe-in-angels/.

Durkheim, Emile. 1915. *The Elementary Forms of the Religious Life*. New York: Free Press.

Eck, Diane. 2002. *A New Religious America: How a "Christian Country" Has Become the World's Most Religiously Diverse Nation*. New York: HarperOne.

Ecklund, Elaine, and Christopher Scheitle 2007. "Religion among Academic Scientists: Distinctions, Disciplines, and Demographics." *Social Problems* 54: 289–307.

Edgell, Penny, Joseph Gerteis, and Douglas Hartmann. 2006. "Atheists as 'Other': Moral Boundaries and Cultural Membership in American Society." *American Sociological Review* 71(2): 211–234.

Ellison, Christopher, Jeffrey Burr, and Patricia McCall 2003. 'The Enduring Puzzle of Southern Homicide.' *Homicide Studies* 7: 326–352.

Epstein, Greg. 2009. *Good without God: What a Billion Nonreligious People Do Believe*. New York: HarperCollins.

Erickson, Joseph. 1992. "Adolescent Religious Development and Commitment: A Structural Equation Model of the Role of the Family, Peer Group, and Educational Influences." *Journal for the Scientific Study of Religion* 31: 131–152.

Everett, Daniel. 2008. *Don't Sleep, There Are Snakes*. New York: Vintage.

Fajnzylber, Oablo, Daniel Lederman, and Norman Loatza 2002. "Inequality and Violent Crime." *Journal of Law and Economics* 45: 1–40.

Fitzpatrick, Frank. 2010. "Keeping the Faith? Not in Vancouver." http://www.philly.com/inquirer/world_us/20100226_Keeping_the_faith__Not_in_Vancouver.html.

Foster, Lawrence. 1984. *Religion and Sexuality: The Shakers, the Mormons, and the Oneida Community*. Urbana: University of Illinois Press.

Fox, James, and Jack Levin. 2000. *The Will to Kill*. Boston, MA: Allyn and Bacon.

Freud, Sigmund. 1961. *The Future of an Illusion*. New York: W. W. Norton.

Froese, Paul. 2008. *The Plot to Kill God: Findings from the Soviet Experiment in Secularization*. Berkeley: University of California Press.

Fulton, Aubyn, Richard Gorsuch, and Elizabeth Maynard. 1999. "Religious Orientation, Antihomosexual Sentiment, and Fundamentalism among Christians." *Journal for the Scientific Study of Religion* 38(1): 14–22.

Gallup, George, Jr., and Jim Castelli. 1989. *The People's Religion*. New York: Macmillan.

Gallup, George, Jr., and D. Michael Lindsay. 1999. *Surveying the Religious Landscape*. Harrisburg, PA: Morehouse.

Giligan, C. 1982. *In a Different Voice*. Cambridge, MA: Harvard University Press.

Ginzburg, Carlo. 1980. *The Cheese and the Worms: The Cosmos of a Sixteenth-Century Miller*. Baltimore: Johns Hopkins University Press.

Glock, Charles. 1967. *To Comfort and to Challenge*. Berkeley: University of California Press.

Goffman, Erving. 1963. *Stigma: Notes on the Management of Spoiled Identity*. New York: Simon and Schuster.

Goldman, Marion. 1999. *Passionate Journeys: Why Successful Women Joined a Cult*. Ann Arbor: University of Michigan Press.

Golumbaski, Denise. 1997. "Prison Incarceration and Religious Preference," http://www.adherents.com/misc/adh_prison.html#altformat.

Gorski, Eric. 2009. "Atheist Student Groups Flowering on Campus." *The Register-Guard*, November 22, p. A6.

Gorski, Philip. 2003. "Historicizing the Secularization Debate: An Agenda for Research," in *Handbook of the Sociology of Religion*, edited by Michele Dillon. New York: Cambridge University Press.

Gottlieb, Anthony. 2008. "Faith Equals Fertility," MoreIntelligentLife. com, http://www.moreintelligentlife.com/story/faith-equals-fertility.

Grasmick, Harold, Elizabeth Davenport, Mitchell Chamlin, and Robert Bursik. 1992. "Protestant Fundamentalism and the Retributive Doctrine of Punishment." *Criminology* 30: 21–45.

Greeley, Andrew. 1972. *Unsecular Man: The Persistence of Religion*. New York: Dell.

Greeley, Andrew, and Michael Hout. 2006. *The Truth about Conservative Christians*. Chicago: University of Chicago Press.

Gross, Neil, and Solon Simmons. 2009. "The Religiosity of American College and University Professors." *Sociology of Religion* 70(2): 101–129.

Grotenhuis, Manfred Te, and Peer Scheepers. 2001. "Churches in Dutch: Causes of Religious Disaffiliation in the Netherlands, 1937–1995." *Journal for the Scientific Study of Religion* 40(4): 591–606.

Grupp, F. W. Jr., and W. M. Newman. 1973. "Political Ideology and Religious Preference: The John Birch Society and Americans for Democratic Action." *Journal for the Scientific Study of Religion* 12: 401–413.

Grus, Joel. 2009. *Your Religion Is False*. Seattle, WA: Brightwalton.

Guth, James, John Green, Lyman Kellstedt, and Corwin Smidt 2005. "Faith and Foreign Policy: A View from the Pews." *Review of Faith and International Affairs* 3: 3–9.

Hadaway, Kirk. 1989. "Identifying American Apostates: A Cluster Analysis." *Journal for the Scientific Study of Religion* 28(2): 201–215.

Hadaway, C. Kirk, and Wade Clark Roof. 1988. "Apostasy in American Churches: Evidence from National Survey Data," in *Falling from the Faith: Causes and Consequences of Religious Apostasy*, edited by David G. Bromley. Newbury Park, CA: Sage.

Hadden, Jeffrey. 1987. "Toward Desacralizing Secularization Theory." *Social Forces* 65: 587–611.

Hale, Russell J. 1980. *The Unchurched: Who They Are and Why They Stay Away*. San Francisco, CA: Harper and Row.

Hamer, Dean. 2004. *The God Gene: How Faith Is Hardwired into Our Genetics*. New York: Doubleday.

Hardy, Sam, and Marcela Raffaelli. 2003. "Adolescent Religiosity and Sexuality: An Investigation of Reciprocal Influences." *Journal of Adolescence* 26: 731–739.

Harper, Marcel. 2007. "The Stereotyping of Nonreligious People by Religious Students: Contents and Subtypes." *Journal for the Scientific Study of Religion* 46(4): 539–552.

Harris, Sam. 2004. *The End of Faith*. New York: W. W. Norton.

Haught, James. 2010. *Fading Faith: The Rise of the Secular Age*. Charleston, WV: Gustav Broukal Press.

Hay, David. 1990. *Religious Experience Today: Studying the Facts*. London: Mowbray.

Hayes, Bernadette. 1995a. "The Impact of Religious Identification on Political Attitudes: An International Comparison." *Sociology of Religion* 56: 177–194.

Hayes, Bernadette. 1995b. "Religious Identification and Moral Attitudes: The British Case." *British Journal of Sociology* 46: 457–474.

Hayes, Bernadette. 2000. "Religious Independents within Western Industrialized Nations: A Socio-Demographic Profile." *Sociology of Religion* 61: 191–207.

Hayes, B., and Y. Pittelkow. 1993. 'Religious Belief, Transmission, and the Family.' *Journal of Marriage and the Family* 55: 755–766.

Hecht, Jennifer Michael. 2003. *Doubt: A History*. San Francisco: HarperCollins.

Hefland, Duke. 2009. "Why Many Americans Change Faiths." *Los Angeles Times,* April 28, p. A12.

Heiner, Robert. 1992. "Evangelical Heathens: The Deviant Status of Freethinkers in Southland." *Deviant Behavior: An Interdisciplinary Journal* 12: 1–20.

Hitchens, Christopher. 2007. *God Is Not Great*. New York: Twelve.

Hoffman, John, and Alan Miller. 1997. "Social and Political Attitudes among Religious Groups: Convergence and Divergence Over Time." *Journal for the Scientific Study of Religion* 36(1): 52–70.

Hood, R.W., Spilka, B., Hunsberger, B., and R.L. Gorsuch. 1996. *The Psychology of Religion: An Empirical Approach*. New York: Guilford.

Hout, Michael. 2003. "Demographic Methods for the Sociology of Religion," in *Handbook of the Sociology of Religion*, edited by Michele Dillon. New York: Cambridge University Press.

Hout, Michael, and Claude Fischer. 2002. "Why More Americans Have No Religious Preference: Politics and Generations." *American Sociological Review* 67(2): 165–190.

Houtman, Dick, and Peter Mascini. 2002. "Why Do Churches Become Empty, While New Age Grows? Secularization and Religious Change in the Netherlands." *Journal for the Scientific Study of Religion* 41(3): 455–474.

Hunsberger, Bruce. 1980. "A Reexamination of the Antecedents of Apostasy." *Review of Religious Research* 21(2): 158–170.

Hunsberger, Bruce. 1983. "Apostasy: A Social Learning Perspective." *Review of Religious Research* 25: 21–38.

Hunsberger, Bruce. 1985. "Parent-University Student Agreement on Religious and Nonreligious Issues." *Journal for the Scientific Study of Religion* 24: 314–320.

Hunsberger, Bruce, and Bob Altemeyer. 2006. *Atheists: A Groundbreaking Study of America's Nonbelievers*. Amherst, NY: Prometheus.

Hunsberger, Bruce, and L. B. Brown. 1984. "Religious Socialization, Apostasy, and the Influence of Family Background." *Journal for the Scientific Study of Religion* 23: 239–251.

Hunt, Stephen. 2005. *Religion and Everyday Life*. London: Routledge.

Hunter, James Davison. 1990. "The Williamsburg Charter Survey: Methodology and Findings." *Journal of Law and Religion* 8: 257–272.

Iannaccone, Laurence. 1990. "Religious Practice: A Human Capital Approach." *Journal for the Scientific Study of Religion* 29: 297–314.

Jacobs, Janet. 1989. *Divine Disenchantment: Deconverting from New Religions*. Bloomington: Indiana University Press.

Jensen, Lene Arnett. 2009. "Conceptions of God and the Devil across the Lifespan: A Cultural-Developmental Study of Religious Liberals and Conservatives." *Journal for the Scientific Study of Religion* 48(1): 121–145.

Jensen, G. F. 2006. "Religious Cosmologies and Homicide Rates among Nations." *The Journal of Religion and Society* 8: 1–13.

Johnson, Carson. 1995. "Formal Education vs. Religious Belief." *Journal for the Scientific Study of Religion* 26: 231–246.

Johnson, Daniel Carson. 1997. "Formal Education vs. Religious Belief: Soliciting New Evidence with Multinomial Logit Modeling." *Journal for the Scientific Study of Religion* 36(2): 231–246.

Johnson, Daniel Carson. 1998. "Apostates Who Never Were: The Social Construction of *Absque Facto* Apostate Narratives," in *The Politics of Religious Apostasy*, edited by David Bromley, pp. 115–138. Westport, CT: Praeger.

Johnson, Miriam. 1991. *Strong Mothers, Weak Wives*. Berkeley: University of California Press.

Kanazawa, Satoshi. 2010. "Why Liberals and Atheists Are More Intelligent." *Social Psychology Quarterly* 73(1): 33–57.

Keysar, Ariela. 2007. "Who Are America's Atheists and Agnostics?" in *Secularism and Secularity: Contemporary International Perspectives*, edited by Barry Kosmin and Ariela Keysar. Hartford, CT: Institute for the Study of Secularism in Society and Culture.

King, Pamela, James Furrow, and Natalie Roth. 2002. "The Influence of Families and Peers on Adolescent Religiousness." *Journal for Psychology and Christianity* 21: 109–120.

King, Pamela, and Ross Mueller. 2004. "Parental Influences on Adolescent Religiousness: Exploring the Roles of Spiritual

Modeling and Spiritual Capital." *Marriage and Family: A Christian Journal* 6: 413–425.

Kleugel, James. 1980. "Denominational Mobility." *Journal for the Scientific Study of Religion* 19: 26–39.

Koenig, Harold, Michael McCullough, and David Larson. 2001. *Handbook of Religion and Health*. New York: Oxford University Press.

Kohlberg, Lawrence. 1973. "The Claim to Moral Adequacy of a Highest Stage of Moral Judgment." *The Journal of Philosophy* 70 (18): 630–646.

Kosmin, Barry. 2009. "The Rising Tide of Secularity." *Freethought Today* 26(10): 8–10.

Kosmin, Barry. 2008. "Areligious, Irreligious and Anti-Religious Americans: The No Religion Population of the U.S.—'Nones.'" http://www.trincoll.edu/secularisminstitute/.

Kosmin, Barry. 2007. "Contemporary Secularity and Secularism," in *Secularism and Secularity: Contemporary International Perspectives*, edited by Barry Kosmin and Ariela Keysar, pp. 1–13. Hartford, CT: Institute for the Study of Secularism in Society and Culture.

Kosmin, Barry, and Keysar, Ariela. 2008. *ARIS 2008 Summary Report*. Trinity College, CT. http://www.americanreligionsurvey-aris.org/.

Kosmin, Barry, and Ariela Keysar. 2007. *Secularism and Secularity: Contemporary International Perspectives*. Hartford, CT: Institute for the Study of Secularism in Society and Culture.

Kosmin, Barry, and Ariela Keysar. 2006. *Religion in a Free Market: Religious and Non-Religious Americans*. Ithaca, NY: Paramount Market.

Kosmin, Barry, and Seymour Lachman. 1993. *One Nation under God: Religion in Contemporary American Society*. New York: Crown.

Kurtz, Paul. 1994. *Living without Religion*. Amherst, NY: Prometheus.

Landsberg, Mitchell. 2010. "Study Finds Less Religious Affiliation in Young Adults." *Los Angeles Times*, February 22, p. AA1.

Larson, E. J., and L. Witham. 1998. "Leading Scientists Still Reject God." *Nature* 394: 313.

Larson, E .J., and L. Witham. 1997. "Scientists Are Still Keeping the Faith." *Nature* 386: 435.

Lawton, Leora, and Regina Bures. 2001. "Parental Divorce and the 'Switching' of Religious Identity." *Journal for the Scientific Study of Religion* 40(1): 99–111.

Leavy, Stanley. 1988. *In the Image of God: A Psychoanalyst's View*. New Haven: Yale University Press.

Lechner, Frank. 1996. "Secularization in the Netherlands?" *Journal for the Scientific Study of Religion* 35(3): 252–264.

Lee, Lois, and Stephen Bullivant. 2010. "Where Do Atheists Come From?" *New Scientist*, March 3, http://www.newscientist.com/article/mg20527506.100-where-do-atheists-come-from.html.

Lewis, C. S. 1952. *Mere Christianity*. New York: HarperCollins.

Lewis, Gregory. 2003. "Black-White Differences in Attitudes Toward Homosexuality and Gay Rights." *Public Opinion Quarterly* 67: 59–78.

Lewy, Guenter. 2008. *"If God Is Dead, Everything Is Permitted?"* New Brunswick, NJ: Transaction.

Linneman, Thomas, and Margaret Clendenen. 2010. "Sexuality and the Sacred," in *Atheism and Secularity, Volume I*, edited by Phil Zuckerman. Santa Barbara, CA: Praeger ABC-CLIO.

Lobdell, William. 2009. *Losing My Religion: How I Lost My Faith Reporting on Religion in America—and Found Unexpected Peace*. New York: Collins.

Lodge, David. 1980. *Souls and Bodies*. New York: Penguin.

Loftus, John. 2008. *Why I Became an Atheist*. Amherst, NY: Prometheus.

Loftus, Jeni. 2001. "America's Liberalization in Attitudes Toward Homosexuality, 1973–1998." *American Sociological Review* 66: 762–782.

Lynn, R. Harvey, J., and Nyborg, H. 2009. "Average Intelligence Predicts Atheism Rates across 137 Nations." *Intelligence* (37): 11–15.

MacArthur, John. 2001. *The Battle for the Beginning: The Bible on Creation and the Fall of Adam*. Nashville, TN: W Publishing.

Maisel, Eric. 2009. *The Atheist's Way: Living Well without Gods*. Novato, CA: New World Library.

Manning, Christel. 2010. "Atheism, Secularity, the Family, and Children," in *Atheism and Secularity, Volume I*, edited by Phil Zuckerman. Santa Barbara, CA: Praeger ABC-CLIO.

Manning, Christel, and Phil Zuckerman, eds. 2005. *Sex and Religion*. Belmont, CA: Wadsworth.

Martin, David. 2005. *On Secularization: Towards a Revised Generalized Theory*. Burlington, VT: Ashgate.

Martin, David. 1978. *A General Theory of Secularization*. New York: Harper and Row.

Marziali, Carl. 2010. "Study Links Religion and Racism," http://usc-news.usc.edu/university/study_links_religion_and_racism.html?view=full.

Mauss, Armand. 1969. "Dimensions of Religious Defection." *Review of Religious Research* 10(3): 128–135.

McAllister, I. 1998. "Religious Change and Secularization: The Transmission of Religious Values in Australia." *Sociological Analysis* 49: 249–263.

McCullough, Michael, and Timothy Smith. 2003. "Religion and Health: Depressive Symptoms and Mortality as Case Studies," in *Handbook of the Sociology of Religion*, edited by Michele Dillon, pp. 190–206. New York: Cambridge University Press.

McGuire, Meredith. 2002. *Religion: The Social Context*. Long Grove, IL: Waveland.

McLeod, Hugh, and Werner Ustorf. 2003. *The Decline of Christendom in Western Europe, 1750–2000*. New York: Cambridge University Press.

Meacham, Jon. 2009. "The End of Christian America." *Newsweek*, April 13, http://www.newsweek.com/id/192583.

Meier, Ann. 2003. "Adolescents' Transition to First Intercourse, Religiosity, and Attitudes about Sex." *Social Forces* 81: 1031–1052.

Miller, Alan, and John Hoffman. 1995. "Risk and Religion: An Explanation of Gender Differences in Religiosity." *Journal for the Scientific Study of Religion* 34: 63–75.

Miller, Alan, and Rodney Stark. 2002. "Gender and Religiousness: Can Socialization Explanations Be Saved?" *The American Journal of Sociology* 107(6): 1399–1423.

Mills, C. Wright. 1959. *The Sociological Imagination*. New York: Oxford University Press.

Mirza, Syed Kamran. 2003. "Floods, Droughts, and Other Natural Calamities," in *Leaving Islam*, edited by Ibn Warraq. Amherst, NY: Prometheus.

Moore, Anderson K., Anne Driscoll, and Laura Duberstein Lindberg. 1998. "A Statistical Portrait of Adolescent Sex, Contraception, and Childbearing." Washington, DC: The National Campaign to Prevent Teen Pregnancy.

Myers, Scott. 1996a. "Families and the Inheritance of Religiosity." *American Sociological Review* 61: 858–866.

Myers, Scott. 1996b. "An Interactive Model of Religiosity Inheritance: The Importance of Family Context." *American Sociological Review* 61: 858–866.

Nall, Jeff. 2010. "Disparate Destinations, Parallel Paths: An Analysis of Contemporary Atheist and Christian Parenting Literature," in *Religion and the New Atheism*, edited by Amarnath Amarasingam. Unpublished manuscript.

Nason-Clark, Nancy. 1997. *The Battered Wife: How Christians Confront Family Violence*. Louisville, KY: Westminster/John Knox.

Nassi, A. 1981. "Survivors of the Sixties: Comparative Psychosocial and Political Development of Former Berkeley Student Activists." *American Psychologist* 36: 753–761.

Nelsen, Hart. 1990. "The Religious Identification of Children of Interfaith Marriages." *Review of Religious Research* 32: 122–134.

Nelson, Lynn. 1988. "Disaffiliation, Desacralization, and Political Values," in *Falling From Faith*, edited by David Bromley, pp. 122–139. Beverly Hills, CA: Sage.

Newport, Frank. 1999. "Americans Today Much More Accepting of a Woman, Black, Catholic, or Jew as President." http://www.gallup.com/poll/3979/Americans-Today-Much-More-Accepting-Woman-Black-Catholic.aspx.

Nielsen, Kai. 1990. *Ethics without God*. Amherst, NY: Prometheus.

Nooney, Jennifer, and Eric Woodrum. 2002. "Religious Coping and Church-Based Social Support as Predictors of Mental Health Outcomes: Testing a Conceptual Model." *Journal for the Scientific Study of Religion* 41(2): 359–368.

Norris, Pippa, and Ronland Inglehart. 2004. *Sacred and Secular: Religion and Politics Worldwide*. New York: Cambridge University Press.

Nyborg, Helmut. 2008. "The Intelligence-Religiosity Nexus: A Representative Study of White Adolescent Americans." *Intelligence* 37(1): 81–93.

Osborne, Lawrence. 1993. *The Poisoned Embrace: A Brief History of Sexual Pessimism*. New York: Pantheon.

Ozorak, Elizabeth Wiess. 1989. "Social and Cognitive Influences on the Development of Religious Beliefs and Commitment in Adolescence." *Journal for the Scientific Study of Religion* 28: 448–463.

Ozorak, Elizabeth Wiess. 1996. "The Power but Not the Glory: How Women Empower Themselves through Religion." *Journal for the Scientific Study of Religion* 35(1): 17–29.

Parrinder, Geoffrey. 1996. *Sexual Morality in the World's Religions*. Oxford: Oneworld.

Pasquale, Frank. 2010. "A Portrait of Secular Group Affiliates," in *Atheism and Secularity, Volume I*, edited by Phil Zuckerman. Santa Barbara, CA: Praeger ABC-CLIO.

Pasquale, Frank. 2007. "Unbelief and Irreligion, Empirical Study and Neglect Of," in *The New Encyclopedia of Unbelief*, edited by Tom Flynn, pp. 760–766. Amherst, NY: Prometheus.

Paul, Gregory. 2009. "The Chronic Dependence of Popular Religiosity upon Dysfunctional Psychosocial Conditions." *Evolutionary Psychology* 7(3): 398–441.

Paul, Gregory. 2005. "Cross-National Correlations of Quantifiable Societal Health with Popular Religiosity and Secularism in the Prosperous Democracies." *Journal of Religion and Society* 7: 1–17.

Paulhus, Delroy. 1984. "Two-Component Models of Socially Desirable Responding." *Journal of Personality and Social Psychology* 46: 598–609.

Paulos, John Alleb. 2008. "How Many Non-Believers?" *Los Angeles Times*, March 4, p. A17.

Perry, Everett, James Davis, and Ruth Doyle. 1980. "Toward a Typology of Unchurched Protestants." *Review of Religious Research* 21: 388–404.

Petersen, Larry, and Gregory Donnenwerth 1998. "Religion and Declining Support for Traditional Beliefs about Gender Roles and Homosexual Rights." *Sociology of Religion* 59: 353–371.

Pinker, Steven. 2002. *The Blank Slate: The Modern Denial of Human Nature*. London: Penguin.

Purcell, S. 1985. "Relation between Religious Orthodoxy and Marital Sexual Functioning." Paper presented at a meeting of the American Psychological Association, Los Angeles, August 25.

Pyle, Ralph. 2006. "Trends in Religious Stratification: Have Religious Group Socioeconomic Distinctions Declined in Recent Decades?" *Sociology of Religion* 67(1): 61–79.

Ranke-Heinemann, Uta. 1992. *Putting Away Childish Things*. San Francisco: HarperCollins.

Regnerus, Mark. 2007. *Forbidden Fruit: Sex and Religion in the Lives of American Teenagers*. New York: Oxford University Press.

Rice, T. W. 2003. "Believe It or Not: Religious and Other Paranormal Beliefs in the United States." *Journal for the Scientific Study of Religion* 42: 95–106.

Roof, Wade Clark, and Kirk Hadaway. 1977. "Shifts in Religious Preference—the Mid Seventies." *Journal for the Scientific Study of Religion* 16: 409–412.

Roof, Wade Clark, and Kirk Hadaway, 1979. "Denominational Switching in the Seventies: Going beyond Stark and Glock." *Journal for the Scientific Study of Religion* 18: 363–379.

Roof, Wade Clark, and William McKinney. 1987. *American Mainline Religion*. New Brunswick, NJ: Rutgers University Press.

Roozen, David. 1980. "Church Dropouts: Changing Patterns of Disengagement and Re-Entry." *Review of Religious Research* 21: 427–450.

Rose, Susan. 2005. "Going Too Far? Sex, Sin, and Social Policy." *Social Forces* 84: 1207–1232.

Rowatt, Wade, J-Ann Tsang, Jessica Kelly, Brooke LaMartina, Michelle McCullers, and April McKinley. 2006. "Associations between Religious Personality Dimensions and Implicit Homosexual Prejudice." *Journal for the Scientific Study of Religion* 45: 397–406.

Sandomirsky, Sharon, and John Wilson. 1990. "Processes of Disaffiliation: Religious Mobility among Men and Women." *Social Forces* 68: 1211–1229.

Saroglou, Vassilis, and Antonio Munoz-Garcia. 2008. "Individual Differences in Religion and Spirituality: An Issue of Personality Traits and/or Values." *Journal for the Scientific Study of Religion* 47(1): 83–101.

Schieman, Scott. 2010. "Socioeconomic Status and Beliefs about God's Influence in Everyday Life." *Sociology of Religion* 71(1): 25–51.

Schlessinger, Laura. 1998. *The Ten Commandments: The Significance of God's Laws in Everyday Life.* New York: Cliff Street Books.

Schnoor, Randal. 2006. "Being Gay and Jewish: Negotiating Intersecting Identities." *Sociology of Religion* 67(1): 43–60.

Scott, Janny, and David Leonhardt. 2005, "Shadow Lines That Still Divide," in *Class Matters*, pp. 1–26. New York: Henry Holt.

Seidman, Steven. 2009. *The Social Construction of Sex.* New York: W. W. Norton.

Shand, Jack. 1998. "The Decline of Traditional Religious Beliefs in Germany." *Sociology of Religion* 59(2): 179–184.

Sharlet, Jeff. 2005. "Soldiers of Christ." *Harpers Magazine*, May.

Sherkat, Darren. 2009. "Religion and Scientific Proficiency." Unpublished paper.

Sherkat, Darren. 2008. "Beyond Belief: Atheism, Agnosticism, and Theistic Certainty in the United States." *Sociological Spectrum* 28: 438–459.

Sherkat, Darren, 2006. "Religion and Verbal Ability." Paper presented at the annual meeting of the American Sociological Association, Montreal, Quebec.

Sherkat, Darren. 2003. "Religious Socialization: Sources of Influence and Influences of Agency," in *Handbook of the Sociology of Religion*, edited by Michele Dillon. New York: Cambridge University Press.

Sherkat, Darren. 2002. "Sexuality and Religious Commitment in the United States: An Empirical Examination." *Journal for the Scientific Study of Religion* 41(2): 313–323.

Sherkat, Darren. 1998. "Counterculture or Continuity? Competing Influences on Baby Boomer's Religious Orientation and Participation." *Social Forces* 76: 1087–1115.

Sherkat, Darren. 1991a. "Leaving the Faith: Testing Theories of Religious Switching Using Survival Models." *Social Science Research* 20: 171–187.

Sherkat, Darren. 1991b. *Religious Socialization and the Family: An Examination of Religious Influences in the Family over the Life Course.* Unpublished PhD dissertation. Department of Sociology, Duke University.

Sherkat, Darren, and Christopher Ellison 1999. "Recent Developments and Current Controversies in the Sociology of Religion." *Annual Review of Sociology* 25: 363–394.

Sherkat, Darren, and John Wilson. 1995. "Preferences, Constraints, and Choices in Religious Markets: An Examination of Religious Switching and Apostasy." *Social Forces* 73: 993–1026.

Sherkat, Darren, Melissa Powell-Williams, and Gregory Maddox. 2007. "Religion, Politics, and Support for Same-Sex Marriage in the United States, 1988–2006." Paper presented at the annual meeting of the American Sociological Association.

Smidt, Corwin. 2005. "Religion and American Attitudes toward Islam and an Invasion of Iraq." *Sociology of Religion* 66: 243–261.

Smith, Christian. 2007. "Why Christianity Works: An Emotions-Focused Phenomenological Account." *Sociology of Religion* 68(2): 165–178.

Smith, Christian, and Melinda Lundquist Denton. 2005. *Soul Searching: The Religious and Spiritual Lives of American Teenagers.* New York: Oxford University Press.

Smith, Jesse. 2010. "Becoming an Atheist in America: Constructing Identity and Meaning from the Rejection of Theism." *Sociology of Religion* 72(1): 1–23.

Southerton, Simon. 2004. *Losing a Lost Tribe: Native Americans, DNA, and the Mormon Church.* Salt Lake City, UT: Signature Books.

Spickard, James. 2007. "Micro/Qualitative Approaches to the Sociology of Religion: Phenomenologies, Interviews, Narratives, and Ethnographies," in *Handbook of the Sociology of Religion*, edited by James A. Beckford and N. Jay Demerath, pp. 121–143. Thousand Oaks, CA: Sage.

Stark, Rodney. 2008. *What Americans Really Believe.* Waco, TX: Baylor University Press.

Stark, Rodney. 2002. "Physiology and Faith: Addressing the 'Universal' Gender Difference in Religious Commitment." *Journal for the Scientific Study of Religion* 41(3): 495–507.

Stark, Rodney. 1999. "Secularization, R.I.P." *Sociology of Religion* 60: 249–273.

Stark, Rodney. 1972. "The Economics of Piety: Religious Commitment and Social Class," in *Issues in Social Inequality*, edited by G. W. Thielbar and S. D. Feldman, pp. 483–503. Boston, MA: Little, Brown.

Stark, Rodney, and Roger Finke. 2000. *Acts of Faith: Explaining the Human Side of Religion*. Berkeley: University of California Press.

Sullins, D. Paul. 2006. "Gender and Religion: Deconstructing Universality, Constructing Complexity." *American Journal of Sociology* 112: 838–880.

Swatos, William, and Daniel Olson. 2000. *The Secularization Debate*. Lanham, MD: Rowman and Littlefield.

Talbot, Margaret. 2008. "Red Sex, Blue Sex: Who Do So Many Evangelical Teenagers Become Pregnant?" *The New Yorker*: http://www.newyorker.com/reporting/2008/11/03/081103fa_fact_talbot.

Tamney, Joseph, Shawn Powell, and Stephen Johnson. 1989. "Innovation Theory and Religious Nones." *Journal for the Scientific Study of Religion* 28(2): 216–229.

Thompson, Edward, and Kathyrn Remmes. 2002. "Does Masculinity Thwart Being Religious? An Examination of Older Men's Religiousness." *Journal for the Scientific Study of Religion* 41(3): 521–532.

Thrower, James. 1979. *The Alternative Tradition: A Study of Unbelief in the Ancient World*. Paris: Mouton De Gruyter.

Tolstoy, Leo. 1959. *On Life and Essays on Religion*, translated by Aylmer Maude. Oxford: Oxford University Press.

Twain, Mark. 1938. *Letters from the Earth*. New York: Harper and Row.

Veevers, J. E., and D. F. Cousineau. 1980. "The Heathen Canadians: Demographic Correlates of Nonbelief." *The Pacific Sociological Review* 23: 199–216.

Walter, Tony. 1990. "Why Are Most Churchgoers Women?" *Vox Evangelica* 20: 73–90.

Walter, Tony, and Grace Davie. 1998. "The Religiosity of Women in the Modern West," *The British Journal of Sociology* 49(4): 640–660.

Warraq, Ibn, ed. 2003. *Leaving Islam: Apostates Speak Out*. Amherst, NY: Prometheus.

Warren, Rick. 2002. *The Purpose Driven Life*. New York: Zondervan.

Weber, Max. 1991 [1922]. *The Sociology of Religion*. Boston: Beacon.

Wilcox, Melissa. 2002. "When Sheila's a Lesbian: Religious Individualism among Lesbian, Gay, Bisexual, and Transgender Christians." *Sociology of Religion* 63(4): 497–513.

Willits, Fern, and Donald Crider. 1989, "Church Attendance and Traditional Religious Beliefs in Adolescence and Young Adulthood: A Panel Study." *Review of Religious Research* 31: 68–81.

Wilson, Bryan. 1966. *Religion in a Secular Society: A Sociological Comment.* London: C. A. Watts.

Wilson, John, and Darren Sherkat. 1994. "Returning to the Fold." *Journal for the Scientific Study of Religion* 33: 148–161.

Winner, Lauren. 2005. *Real Sex: The Naked Truth about Chastity.* Grand Rapids, MI: Brazos.

Winston, Hella. 2005. *Unchosen: The Hidden Lives of Hasidic Rebels.* Boston: Beacon.

Winter, Miriam Therese, Adair Lummis, and Allison Stokes. 1994. *Defecting in Place: Women Claiming Responsibility for Their Own Spiritual Lives.* New York: Crossroad.

Wolkomir, Michelle. 2006. *Be Not Deceived: The Sacred and Sexual Struggles of Gay and Ex-Gay Christian Men.* New Brunswick, NJ: Rutgers University Press.

Wright, Stuart. 1991. "Reconceptualizing Cult Coercion and Withdrawal: A Comparative Analysis of Divorce and Apostasy." *Social Forces* 70(1): 125–145.

Wrong, Dennis. 1961. "The Over-Socialized Conception of Man in Modern Sociology." *American Sociological Review* 26: 184–193.

Wuthnow, Robert. 1989. *The Struggle for America's Soul: Evangelicals, Liberals, and Secularism.* Grand Rapids, MI: Eerdmans.

Wuthnow, Robert, and Charles Glock. 1973. "Religious Loyalty, Defection, and Experimentation among College Youth." *Journal for the Scientific Study of Religion* 12(2): 157–180.

Wuthnow, Robert, and Glen Mellinger. 1978. "The Religiosity of College Students: Stability and Change over Years at University." *Journal for the Scientific Study of Religion* 17: 159–164.

Yamane, David. 1997. "Secularization on Trial." *Journal for the Scientific Study of Religion* 26(1): 109–122.

Yip, Andrew. 2002. "The Persistence of Faith among Nonheterosexual Christians: Evidence for the Neosecularization Thesis of Religious Transformation." *Journal for the Scientific Study of Religion* 41(2): 199–212.

Yip, Andrew. 1997. "Dare to Differ: Gay and Lesbian Catholics' Assessment of Official Catholic Positions on Sexuality." *Sociology of Religion* 58(2): 165–180.

Zelan, Joseph. 1968. "Religious Apostasy, Higher Education, and Occupational Choice," *Sociology of Education* 41(4): 370–379.

Zuckerman, Phil. 2009a. "Atheism, Secularity, and Well-Being: How the Findings of Social Science Counter Negative Stereotypes and Assumptions." *Sociology Compass* 3(6): 949–971.

Zuckerman, Phil. 2009b. "Why Are Danes and Swedes So Irreligious?" *Nordic Journal of Religion and Society* 22(1): 55–69.

Zuckerman, Phil. 2008. *Society without God: What the Least Religious Nations Can Tell Us about Contentment*. New York: New York University Press.

Zuckerman, Phil. 2004. "Secularization: Europe—Yes; United States—No." *Skeptical Inquirer* 28(2): 49–52.

Zuckerman, Phil. 2003. *Invitation to the Sociology of Religion*. New York: Routledge.

Zuckerman, Phil, ed. 2000. *Du Bois on Religion*. Walnut Creek, CA: AltaMira.

INDEX